Praise for

The
Tapping
Solution
for
Teenage Girls

'It has been said that the emotional wounds of high school have the half-life of uranium. In my decades of medical practice, I've seen the adverse effects of these wounds years later — in the minds, spirits and emotions of adult women. But this doesn't have to be the case. The Tapping Solution for Teenage Girls provides teenage girls with precisely the tools they need to regularly and effectively discharge the emotional stress of their intense lives. As a result, girls have the opportunity to reach adulthood as whole, confident women — unencumbered by a lot of baggage from their teen years. I highly recommend this book to anyone who has a teenage daughter or who cares about one.'

— Dr Christiane Northrup, New York Times bestselling author of Women's Bodies, Women's Wisdom and Goddesses Never Age

'Oh, how I wish I had this book when I was a teenager! The angst, the stress, the confusion, so much of it is cleared up in this fantastic guide, and most importantly, the incredible resource of EFT is explained in wonderful detail. I can't go back in time, but I will share this book with all the teenage girls I know!'

— Kris Carr, New York Times bestselling author

'This is the book everyone out of their teens wishes they had as a teenager! Chris Wheeler is making that wish come true for a new generation of teens. The Tapping Solution for Teenage Girls is relatable, easy to follow and transformational. The best part is knowing this information will not only help you now, but for years to come.'

— Jessica Ortner, author of The Tapping Solution for Weight Loss and Body Confidence

'I will use this book in my medical practice for every teen! Teenage anxiety is a huge cause of teen illness and disease as an adult. This is by far the most useful book I've come across to support teens and really call out the disturbing thoughts they haven't been able to communicate to anyone. This book will change the lives of millions!'

— Kim D'Eramo, D.O., ABEM board-certified emergency physician and founder of the American Institute of Mind Body Medicine

The Tapping Solution
for
Teenage Girls

ALSO BY CHRISTINE WHEELER

IBS for Dummies

The IBS Cookbook for Dummies

The Tapping Solution for Teenage Girls

Christine Wheeler

HAY HOUSE

Carlsbad, California • New York City • London • Sydney
Johannesburg • Vancouver • Hong Kong • New Delhi

First published and distributed in the United Kingdom by:
Hay House UK Ltd, Astley House, 33 Notting Hill Gate, London W11 3JQ
Tel: +44 (0)20 3675 2450; Fax: +44 (0)20 3675 2451; www.hayhouse.co.uk

Published and distributed in the United States of America by:
Hay House Inc., PO Box 5100, Carlsbad, CA 92018-5100
Tel: (1) 760 431 7695 or (800) 654 5126
Fax: (1) 760 431 6948 or (800) 650 5115; www.hayhouse.com

Published and distributed in Australia by:
Hay House Australia Ltd, 18/36 Ralph St, Alexandria NSW 2015
Tel: (61) 2 9669 4299; Fax: (61) 2 9669 4144; www.hayhouse.com.au

Published and distributed in the Republic of South Africa by:
Hay House SA (Pty) Ltd, PO Box 990, Witkoppen 2068
info@hayhouse.co.za; www.hayhouse.co.za

Published and distributed in India by:
Hay House Publishers India, Muskaan Complex, Plot No.3, B-2,
Vasant Kunj, New Delhi 110 070
Tel: (91) 11 4176 1620; Fax: (91) 11 4176 1630; www.hayhouse.co.in

Distributed in Canada by:
Raincoast Books, 2440 Viking Way, Richmond, B.C. V6V 1N2
Tel: (1) 604 448 7100; Fax: (1) 604 270 7161; www.raincoast.com

Text © 2016 by Christine Wheeler

Indexer: Joan Shapiro • Cover design: Michelle Polizzi • Interior design: Pamela Homan • Interior illustrations: Tapping Points (page 20): Courtesy of Nick Ortner • Finger Tapping Points (page 25): Illustration by Pia Edberg

The moral rights of the author have been asserted.

A catalogue record for this book is available from the British Library.

ISBN: 978-1-78180-620-3

Printed and bound in Great Britain by TJ International Ltd, Padstow

For teenage girls of
yesterday, today and tomorrow

CONTENTS

FOREWORD

When Chris Wheeler first approached me with the idea to write a tapping book for teenage girls, I had a secret. My wife, Brenna, was pregnant, and our first child, a girl, would be born the following spring. Publishing a book that could someday help our child, as well as our niece, all the while supporting today's teens, felt like a no-brainer.

For girls and boys alike, the teenage years are a time of intense, rapid growth. Oftentimes, the emotional, social, mental, and physical changes pile on top of each other so quickly that they, and the adults who love and care for them, feel overwhelmed. Although they may need, even yearn, to share their emotions, teenagers are often too consumed with everything they're experiencing to do that. If, by publishing this book, we can support teenage girls with the unique challenges they face, why wouldn't we do that?

I'm thrilled to share that the book that resulted from that commitment exceeds even my original hopes. After years of working with adults who struggle with emotional residue from their own teenage years, I see this book also as a way to support teenage girls' future selves. Rather than dragging painful memories and heavy emotions into adulthood, this book will guide them through a process of shedding challenges *as they're happening.* In short, thanks to Chris's expert guidance, this book will help teenage girls to thrive now and in their future adult lives.

One of the things that also excites me about this book is how perfectly suited tapping is to teenagers. In addition to providing powerful relief quickly, tapping is a tool they can use on their own at any time, whether at home, in class, or in a bathroom stall. It's truly a tool that teenage girls can use when, where, and how they choose.

Thanks to her extensive experience working with teenage girls, Chris has done a fantastic job of navigating the many challenges these girls face. I'm excited and honored to introduce this book for teenage girls and the many adults who love and nurture them.

Nick Ortner

New York Times best-selling author of
The Tapping Solution and *The Tapping Solution for Pain Relief*

INTRODUCTION:
This Is Your Book!

Hi, my name is Christine and I've written this book for you.

If you're like me when I was a teenage girl, you probably have some stress in your life. As a teen, I was supersensitive and often told I was moody, grumpy, snippy, and so on. I would cry at the drop of a hat, and I felt misunderstood because I was told that whatever had just made me cry shouldn't have made me cry. I wish I'd known about the awesome stress-relieving technique called tapping then. What a relief it would have been to go to my room and tap through those tears, instead of feeling worse because someone in my family was saying things like this to me:

- Just calm down about it.
- It's not a big deal.
- Stop being so dramatic.
- You're too sensitive.
- It's not the end of the world.
- Other people have *real* problems.

But tapping—or Emotional Freedom Techniques (EFT), as it's formally known—wasn't developed until the early 1990s, and I finally learned it in 2000. When I did, I tapped about everything I could think of. I quickly realized that many of the issues and feelings I was tapping about had something to do with things that had happened when I was a teenager! I was really impressed with how much better I felt about those things after tapping, and about day-to-day stuff as well. I couldn't wait to share it with people, so I did some tapping with friends and co-workers. Eventually I left my job and began tapping with people full-time. Over the years, I've worked with thousands of people and here's the thing that always shocked me: almost every woman I worked with was still upset and stressed about something that had happened when she was a teenage girl!

I kept thinking how much better life would have been for lots of women if they'd known how to tap when they were your age. I know you're not thinking that far ahead—so I'm doing it for you! By tapping today on things that are bothering you today, you'll reduce your stress right now and in the future.

What Is Tapping, Anyway?

You know how sometimes you'll put your head in your hands when you're upset? Or your hand across your forehead, or across the middle of your chest, when something shocks or startles you? Try this right now. These are all ways that we naturally calm ourselves. I think our cavewomen ancestors did the same things. Sometimes we cross our arms in front of us—kind of giving ourselves a hug—or drum our fingers on the table when we're nervous. Even Tarzan thumped on a spot in the middle of his chest to feel more powerful.

Tapping is just another, more specific way of using the natural power of touch to soothe and heal. It's a simple technique you can use whenever you want to feel calmer or lift your energy. When you tap, you'll be using your fingertips to actually *tap* on specific points on your own face, head, and body while repeating specific words and phrases. You can do tapping in private or in public, and if you feel self-conscious about tapping when there are people around, I'll show you a way to do it so subtly that no one will know what you're up to! With tapping, the power to give yourself more calmness, energy, and strength is literally in your hands.

About This Book

This is your book! Even if someone who cares about you—a parent or a guardian, an aunt or an uncle, a teacher or a neighbor—bought you this book in hopes that you would feel better, this book is written for you. And if you found this book on your own . . . well, you *know* it's for you! So please keep reading, because I'm going to tell you about some super easy relaxation techniques you can do by yourself to help you stop freaking out about stuff that's happening in your life and get back to being your awesome self. I'm sure you'll be able to relate to the stories I'm sharing from teenage girls who've been using tapping to do just that. (The names in the book have been changed so they remain anonymous.)

Part One of the book tells you what you need to know to use the rest of the book. Please start there. Chapter 1 talks about stress, what it is, and how it affects you. I'll explain how you're probably carrying around a pretty full "stress backpack," and how most people carry their full stress backpacks into their adult lives.

In Chapter 2 you'll learn how to do this tapping stuff I've been talking about. You'll catch on to it right away and probably start feeling better quickly.

Chapter 3 is awesome because it gives you a deep understanding of all the events, thoughts, feelings, and actions you can tap on to give you great relief from stress in all areas of your life. Then the rest of the book talks about day-to-day things that happen in the lives of teenage girls, and how to use these techniques to feel better about them.

Part Two is all about your body and your mind, and I can tell you that you'll be relieved to learn how to tap on some of these topics! A lot of this stuff can be hard for girls to talk about, so you'll have the privacy to tap about it on your own instead. Chapter 4 starts right in with guiding you through some inspirational tapping about your body, your appearance, and how you feel about yourself. Chapter 5 covers "that time of the month," and you'll get to tap about the symptoms, discomfort, and emotional upset that can accompany your monthly visitor. And in Chapter 6, I'll look at the emotional stuff that happens for so many teenage girls. This chapter will feature lots of tapping to boost your emotional health and calm anxiety, fear, grief, and so on.

In Part Three, you'll be surprised by how much you'll learn about tapping solutions for stuff that happens at home. We'll talk about the upset of parents fighting and divorcing and how to tap through the stress of those life challenges in Chapter 7. In Chapter 8 you'll learn powerful tapping secrets to use to ease some of the conflicts you may be having with your parents. If you have siblings, you might have some conflicts with them too, and Chapter 9 will help you get through those.

Part Four is all about stuff that happens at school, and after school. Chapter 10 focuses on helping you tap about your schoolwork, homework, test anxiety, and distractions. Chapter 11 will help you deal with the pressure you may feel about grades, report cards, and college, whether that's coming from your parents, your teachers, or yourself. If you've had any experience being bullied, teased, or gossiped about, that's a horrible thing for you to go through, and I hope that the exercises in Chapter 12 will give you some peace of mind and help you get your power back. And in addition to all the stuff that happens at school, Chapter 13 is meant to help you get over the challenges you might have in activities outside of school—sports, the arts, music, acting, drawing—and help you do your best at the things you enjoy. I hope that this chapter helps you get closer and closer to fulfilling your dreams.

Part Five is about relationships and how to navigate the stressful situations they can create. In Chapter 14, we'll talk about friendships, making friends, wanting to be liked . . . and even feeling rejected. Then, in Chapter 15, you'll be able to practice tapping about romantic relationships, crushes, breakups, and even what to do when someone you like doesn't like you back. All the stuff in this chapter on romantic relationships is for girls who might like boys . . . and for girls who might like girls. Finally, in Chapter 16, I'll talk about how normal it is to have sexual feelings. You'll be able to explore any discomfort you might have and feel better about your natural curiosity.

Then, at the end of the book, there's a whole bonus part called "There's More to Explore." Here you'll find even more tapping solutions for the stuff that's happening in all these areas of your life.

To sum up each of the tapping chapters, I've shared a tapping affirmation, or what I call a Tapfirmation. A Tapfirmation is a single, positive statement for you to repeat while tapping the tapping points. Tapping while repeating a positive statement can help reinforce the good feeling you've achieved while tapping throughout the chapter. I also tweet Tapfirmations on Twitter (@TapWithChris) and post them on Instagram (@tapwithchristine) to help you tap into the positive.

How to Use This Book

Remember that this is your book—your personal guide to feeling better about the things that are bothering you. The first thing I want you to do is get yourself a notebook, journal, sketch pad, diary, or some pieces of paper, and a pen or pencil. You'll want to write stuff down as we go along. Sometimes I'll ask you to write down words that describe how you feel, or what you think about something. So have pen and paper handy when you start reading the pages ahead.

If you haven't already looked at the Index of this book, flip to it now. You'll see an alphabetical index of terms and topics that are discussed throughout the book. Where there's a page number given in boldface type, it means there's a tapping script about that issue on that page. You can go through the Index and make a note of the items that you want to investigate further and maybe tap on. You can mark them right there on the pages—yes, I give you permission to write in this beautiful book!—or you can write the items and page numbers down in your notebook. Once you're comfortable with the technique of tapping (which is super easy!), you'll be able to apply it to these items and anything else that comes up in your life.

In just a minute, we'll get started. First, though, I want you to meet Cassidy, my amazing teen consultant who's been helping me with this book since the beginning. Cassidy approved the topics that you'll find in this book, and she also hops in every once in a while with a note or a tip (they're called Cassidy's Comments) to help you get the most out of the book and to have an awesome experience with tapping.

. . . .

INTRODUCTION FROM CASSIDY

Hi, my name is Cassidy and as I'm writing this, I'm 16 years old, heading into 12th grade. I've been doing EFT tapping since I was seven, when I met Christine, the author of this book (I call her Chris). My mom and Chris are friends, and my mom had just learned about tapping from Chris.

I don't even remember the first thing Chris and I tapped on. I just know that tapping instantly became a part of our lives. Anytime I was upset about something, my mom would remind me to tap and I'd say, "Oh yeah." I'd tap and instantly feel better. It is hard to explain what tapping has done for me; half of the things I have done, like getting up on a stage or getting through something difficult, I probably either wouldn't have done as well or wouldn't have done at all. We have made tapping into a habit that we've kept ever since.

One day Chris came over when we'd just moved into a house and our dogs were going crazy, barking constantly. We thought it would be funny to try tapping on the dogs and we could not believe that they calmed right down. A few minutes later, when my grandma came to the house, she wondered where the dogs were because they didn't make a peep when she came to the door. Believe me, that was a miracle.

So if you're hesitating to learn this awesome technique for yourself, think about helping your parents or your pets! But tapping will work for you. It grounds you and helps you realize that you will be all right no matter what the situation.

Tapping helped me with so many things that I really wished everyone knew about it, but let's face it, it sounds kind of weird. Can you imagine saying to your friend, "Hey, Katherine, feeling stressed about exams? Just tap on your face and say a few things and it will set you free!" Chris asked me if I thought having a book in their hands would help teenage girls use tapping. I immediately knew it was a great idea. If girls could do this on their own, without it coming from their parents as a therapy sort of thing, they would get so many benefits. Then she asked me if I'd like to be her Teen Consultant. I told her would be happy to help her, since I have tapped for most of my life. I knew how much it helped me and I am so happy to be able to help other girls get the kind of comfort, calmness, and confidence that I've gotten from tapping.

I also know how important this book is to Chris, who wants to help all the people she hasn't gotten the chance to help face-to-face. That's one of the things I really appreciate about working on things with Chris. No matter how young I was or how insignificant my "stuff" may have seemed to most adults, Chris always understood and treated everything like a big deal. Which it was to me at the time—at least until I tapped on it! She doesn't talk down or patronize, and you'd think she has faced every single problem imaginable the way she gets it. And she never acts like she knows better. She is all about arming you with the tools to tackle anything that comes your way, not hoarding the answer so she can be the hero. That is what is so amazing about this book. It feels like she's sharing her superpower with everyone!

I know your parents or some other adult probably gave you this book, telling you to do the exercises in it so you can stop stressing about your life. And I also know you might be rebelling about reading the book; I probably wouldn't want to read a "get rid of stress" book if my parents gave me one either. But this isn't some pointless book that should sit at the back of your bookshelf. Stress really sucks; it's something that no one wants to carry with them. I know sometimes drama can be kind of exciting and give you a temporary thrill. I have had my share of drama too! I know the thrilling few hours of being involved in a circle of madness that makes you feel like your life is as interesting as the characters in *Gossip Girl*, but honestly, wouldn't you rather feel calmer about school, family stuff, crushes, sports, or performances?

So trust me on this—you will want to try EFT tapping. I know it seems kind of weird, and it was pretty funny to me when I first did it, but I actually felt better, calmer, and less distracted by the stuff that was stressing me—*as soon as I did it*. I'm not kidding; I mean literally right after I did it. Now I use EFT tapping all the time and it's helped me in basketball, with acting, and I've even written and performed my own songs with just a little bit of nervousness. EFT tapping has calmed my anxiety and helped me really enjoy things that most people think are terrifying. Like I said, it's almost as if you have a worry-free superpower.

Please give this book and tapping a try. Read and tap through these exercises that I've approved personally for you. Have fun with it. It really will help you; I cannot express in words how much it has helped me. But you have to do it for it to help!

A Note to Parents, Caregivers, and Caring Adults

Thank you for finding this book for the teenage girl in your life. If you've ever thought, *I wish there was something I could do to help her*, this book is an answer to your plea. When your daughter is hurting, you hurt. You may find that you feel overwhelmed by her pain. Your love, support, understanding, and compassion are invaluable to her as she goes through difficult times, but the truth is, there is only so much you can do. After all, what she's feeling is her experience, her truth, and her challenge to face.

If you've ever felt helpless watching your daughter or a teenage girl you care about suffer, this book offers a new solution for both of you. Giving her this book puts a choice into her hands and a new, self-empowering tool literally at her fingertips. This book gives her the opportunity to take charge of the unhelpful thoughts, feelings, and hurts that may be upsetting and even overwhelming her. It acknowledges, honors, and demystifies her sometimes scary emotions and gives her tools she can use immediately to find a more peaceful place in her body, mind, and spirit.

Tapping is a do-it-yourself technique that can help support girls in dealing with anything and everything, but for some issues, girls also need support of a different kind. Tapping is not meant to replace medical or professional care but to complement it.

part one

IMPORTANT STUFF ABOUT STRESS AND TAPPING

. . . .

CASSIDY'S COMMENT

Okay, here we go! You're starting this awesome book and it's best to start at the beginning. In Chapter 1 you're going to find out all about stress, and I love this part because it is proof that teenage girls *are* stressed out. It's not your imagination that sometimes things feel overwhelming.

Then you discover Chapter 2, where Chris shows you all about the tapping technique to help you stop freaking out and keep being awesome! I think you'll really like that because you get an instant thing to do to help you feel better. It's instant, it's easy, and it actually works.

Then Chapter 3 is the answer to your question "What do I tap on?" Spoiler alert: tap on anything! Seriously, anything, no matter how random it seems. Reading this chapter will get you ready to apply tapping to anything and everything that's going on in your life.

. . . .

So even if reading isn't your thing, read this. But don't look at it as work; look at it as finding the keys to the magic kingdom of feeling better about yourself and getting confident, happy, and strong!

chapter 1

WHY AM I FREAKING OUT?

You know when you tell your friend that you're freaking out about something? You're talking about stress. Your parents might be telling you that they're anxious about money, work, or a promotion they're competing for. They're talking about stress too.

Stress describes the feelings and reactions you have to challenging things that are happening. These challenging things and events are called *stressors*. You might say you're stressed about a test that's coming up, the first day of school, or your dance recital. Those are normal, everyday kinds of stresses. We can call this *good stress* because as you learn to handle and manage it, you learn strategies and skills that will help you deal with challenges in the future. Ideally your parents, or other adults, are showing you how to sort out stress. But even good stress can feel like a lot to handle.

A bigger kind of stress, called *tolerable stress*, can be a result of going through life-changing or even life-threatening events, like parents divorcing, an illness, or an accident. These kinds of events can feel pretty extreme, but they have an ending, and hopefully you have the support and guidance of parents or caregivers to help you move through them. Naturally you'll learn new skills when going through this kind of stress too.

If you've been dealing with a horribly stressful situation over a long period of time, maybe with little help from adults, you may be experiencing what experts call *toxic stress*. Teenage girls who have toxic stress may have experienced abuse or neglect or an ongoing difficult home life. If you've experienced bullying over a long period of time, I think that can feel like toxic stress. Toxic stress is very difficult to deal with in general, and it's especially hard to handle it on your own.[1] If you're in a situation at home, at school, or anywhere else that feels unsafe or that you just don't want to cope with all by yourself, I encourage you to talk to a parent, a teacher, a counselor, or an adult friend whom you trust.

It is my hope that you will use the easy exercises I'm going to show you to manage your stress levels so they don't ever become toxic for you.

How Stressed Are You?

Do you think your friends are totally stressed out? Do you worry about your own stress levels? In 2013, a group of researchers gathered information from a thousand teenagers who answered questions online about their stress. The teens reported that their own stress levels are higher than they think is healthy, they feel like their stress is getting worse, and they expect it to just keep getting worse in the next year. And, in case you were wondering, teenage girls' stress levels were higher than those of teenage boys, often making them feel angry, irritable, and on the verge of tears. What's more, most of the girls in this study said that they don't think they're doing a good job managing their stress. Does this describe you?

How Are You Learning to Manage Stress?

You might be getting some relaxation tips from teachers or coaches, but most teenage girls learn from watching their parents and what they do when they're stressed. What are you learning at home? Maybe your parents watch TV or go online as a way to de-stress, or maybe they do yoga, go for walks, or exercise. Maybe they even do some tapping! Whatever your parents do about stress, you're probably doing as well. But the survey I mentioned was pretty clear that teenage girls need to have some solid skills of their own to relieve stress, stop freaking out, and keep being awesome. I promise you that reading this book and doing these easy exercises will be a big help. But you have to do the exercises for them to work!

Your Stress Backpack

Stress is a natural part of everyday life, but it can accumulate. Imagine that you gather up and store your stress (even good stress) in a backpack that you have to carry around with you all the time. Picture your backpack now. What color is it? How big is it? What do you think could be in there? Here are some stressors that might be in your backpack at this very moment:

- An upsetting event
- Schoolwork
- Self-doubt
- An argument with a friend
- A rumor someone's spreading about you
- A rumor you've spread about someone else
- Sadness after a breakup
- Worry about an upcoming exam and/or school project
- Upset about getting grounded for something you did
- An important social event

How many things on this list are you dealing with right now? What would you add to the list? I want you to think about your own list of stressors for a minute. Grab your notebook and write them down. There may be a few or a lot of them. Don't judge the things you put on your list! This is your list and you get to add whatever you want.

Accumulating Stress

Imagine that you put everything on your list into your backpack and carry it around day and night. Heavy, right? Imagine if your stress backpack were a real backpack, loaded with the books you carried to school yesterday. Then, without unloading it, you put in the books you need for today. And then, because you're thinking about the test you have next week, you load all those books in your backpack as well. Now imagine trying to carry that thing around.

It's the same with your stress backpack. If you don't do something to unload the stress that's already in there, as soon as you add another worrisome thing—such as your first date with someone you like, a pop quiz, or even a pimple—that backpack of stress gets heavier and heavier. Even if it's good stress, like a first date or an upcoming party or dance, it's still stress and it adds a weight to your backpack. So if you're feeling overwhelmed, it's probably not just what's happening today that's bothering you—it's probably an accumulation of everything in your backpack.

How Heavy Is Your Stress Backpack?

I want you to imagine what your stress backpack feels like right now. How much stuff are you carrying around with you? When is the last time you cleared it out? How does it feel to know that all that stress is piling up in your backpack? If you like to visualize things, maybe you can see it bulging at the sides and pulling at the zipper. Or maybe your stress backpack is lightweight and manageable!

Maybe there's stuff in your backpack that dates back pretty far. In fourth grade I had a horrible teacher named Miss Campbell, and now I know that she was a major cause of stress when I was 10 years old. Miss Campbell was mean and most of the kids were terrified of her. She often humiliated them in class if they gave a wrong answer. Of course I didn't know anything about stress then; I was 10! But I knew that I didn't want to go to school, and I knew that I was afraid of my teacher, and on school days, I had stomachaches every morning. When I started learning about tapping, I realized that I had been carrying my stress about Miss Campbell around since I was 10. It's like that gross sandwich from weeks ago that you forgot about in your backpack. I had this awful Miss Campbell sandwich weighing down my backpack and oozing stress all over everything.

With the tapping exercises that I'm going to show you, you can begin to unload your backpack of stress (including any forgotten sandwiches) and then have fun filling it up with joyful, positive thoughts, feelings, and ideas. I'm going to show you how to lighten the load and spend more time feeling calm and peaceful, happy and awesome.

How Do You Know You're Stressed?

You probably already know that just thinking about something can feel stressful. Jenny was stressed because she knew she had to tell her friend that she didn't want to spend spring break with her and her family. She knew that her friend would be upset and hurt, and in her mind, Jenny was rehearsing about a hundred different things to say. It was taking up a lot of room in her mind, and her backpack, and it was freaking her out. Jenny wasn't even having the conversation yet, but her palms were already getting sweaty and she was getting a headache.

Does this sound familiar? Do you remember just thinking about something, like an exam or a difficult conversation, and feeling like your brain was full of this problem and your body was tensing up? I know it's super uncomfortable, but it's also normal. And this tapping stuff I've been talking about will help you release these stressful thoughts and calm the tense feelings in your body.

What's Happening in Your Mind When You're Stressed?

Lots of people know they're stressed because they can't stop thinking about something—an event, a person, a problem. Does that sound like you? You might be trying to focus on homework, but your mind keeps going over and over the thing your friend said that bugged you that day. What's going on in your mind is that you are thinking. I'm sure you've said, "I can't stop thinking about _____ !" When you can't stop thinking about something, and you're not resolving the problem, that's stressful!

Mia couldn't stop thinking about what happened!

Mia couldn't believe it. She looked around to see if there were any witnesses, but nobody had seen or heard Stacy, the popular, mean girl, bump into Mia in the hallway and say, "Move it." While Mia stood there stunned, Stacy just kept walking and was long gone before Mia knew what hit her.

Mia went to her next class, but she had a hard time paying attention because she kept playing the event over and over in her head. It was only a few seconds of time, but Mia went over it for easily an hour. *She couldn't stop thinking about it.*

When an event happens, the first thing we do is think about it. It's automatic and it's nature's way of trying to figure out what's going on. What do you think Mia's thoughts were? She thought about it for an hour, so you know she didn't just think, *Oh, whatever* and move on.

Here's a bunch of stuff that Mia could have been thinking:

1. That was so weird.

2. She seems upset; I wonder if she's okay.

3. What a b*#@h!

4. I can't believe she just bashed into me that way!

5. Wait till my girls hear about this.

6. What did I ever do to her?

7. Oh crap, does this mean she's going to start picking on me?

8. What if she singles me out?

9. What am I going to do?

10. Why didn't I say something? Why didn't I say sorry?

11. She's in my next class—how can I avoid her?

12. Should I say something to her?

13. OMG, I can't believe this is happening!

14. Why does stuff like this always happen to me?

Okay, you can see the pile of thoughts that you can have after one brief encounter with someone in the hallway. Mia hasn't even told anyone yet, but her thoughts have moved way past "Oh, whatever." Her mind is racing, she can't focus in class, and she's feeling more and more stressed. She's already packing this away in her backpack.

And—this is super important—when she's going through a list of 14 thoughts like this, she doesn't have a lot of room to think about the awesome things she'd rather be thinking about.

I know you can't stop thinking,
but with tapping, you can change your thinking!

How Does Your Body Feel When You're Stressed?

After the hour of ruminating in class, it was lunchtime, but Mia's stomach was churning and she had no appetite. Her head hurt from thinking so much about the event with Stacy. Again, it's uncomfortable but perfectly normal for your body to have a reaction when you're upset (though that doesn't mean it always will). Maybe you're like me and Mia and you get a stomachache, or maybe you know you're stressed when these other symptoms show up:

- Headache
- Dry mouth
- Heart racing
- Sweating or sweaty palms
- Hunger
- No appetite
- Trouble sleeping

Even though it's normal to have reactions to things that happen, if you don't have a way to release your reaction (think: tapping), the stress may land in your body. Very often you'll notice that you have a feeling in your body at the same time you have a worry in your mind. Remember I told you about my very scary fourth-grade teacher, Miss Campbell? I was so stressed about going to school to face that teacher-zilla that I got stomachaches and so I was able to stay home from school a fair bit. As soon as the school day started and I was still at home in my pajamas watching cartoons, my stomachache went away. But the stress never really got resolved, and I kept getting stomachaches, and I kept missing school. When my mother took me to the doctor, it turned out that I'd developed an ulcer.

I'm not saying that every stressful situation is going to make you sick, but researchers are connecting stress to physical illness. And the researchers in that stress study I told you about really want teenage girls to find ways to deal with their stress so that the stress doesn't affect their health. I'm sure that if I'd known about tapping when I was dealing with Miss Campbell, I wouldn't have ended up with an ulcer.

Fight or Flight

When you're startled, scared, or freaked out, your body, because it's a genius, gets to work instantly to protect you from whatever just scared you. When your heart starts beating faster and your hands get sweaty, you're heading into fight-or-flight mode. That means your body and mind think you're in some kind of danger, and your body's chemicals and hormones start flowing so you can either stand and fight your enemy or take flight from the dangerous scene you're facing.

Now, this is a natural response that our cave-grandparents developed to deal with the wild tiger lurking around their cave. Do they club the tiger (fight) or do they run from the tiger (flight)? It's natural and it's instinctive and it happens automatically without your thinking about it.

Remember when I talked about stress accumulating? I think when our backpacks are full of stress already and then, like Mia, we get bumped in the hallway, our natural fight-or-flight mechanism goes haywire because we don't have room to carry the weight of another upset. And when something surprising happens, it can instantly feel like too much to deal with. Mia couldn't help but act like Stacy was a menacing tiger, even though she was just another teenage girl.

I know I said earlier that there is such a thing as good stress, because you learn new skills when you face challenges. But too much stress is not good for you. Everyone has a different capacity for stress—a different-sized backpack. No matter how big and heavy your own backpack, I have a way for you to easily identify and neutralize the thoughts and feelings and reactions that can go along with stress. You can see why I want to share this with you, right?

So wouldn't it be a great idea to take a look at your stress backpack and begin emptying it out? Not only will you feel better now, but you'll also have a lifelong tool to use when stress creeps into your life. I'm not saying that your life will be stress-free, because stuff is always happening around us, but you will be better able to neutralize the stress, especially if you start practicing now.

Teen Stress in Your Adult Backpack

Remember I was just telling you about Mia who got bumped in the hallway by Stacy, the popular girl? When she came to see me to learn tapping, she was 30 years old. She was 16 when it happened but Mia had never really gotten over this event. This bump in the hallway became the oozing sandwich in Mia's backpack. Are there things that you've never gotten over? What do I mean by that?

When Mia was bumped in the hallway, she froze for a moment. You've had that happen, right? Something startles you or shocks you so much that you freeze on the spot for a second or two. Then you go about your day. Sometimes, like Mia, you have a moment of freezing and then you sit with your thoughts, ruminating for the next hour or more about the event.

When I met Mia 14 years after the event, she said she was always worried that something bad was going to happen, that someone was out to get her. We talked a bit about this and did some tapping on the current feelings she was having. She didn't know why but said she often felt anxious, upset, uneasy, vulnerable, and sometimes even panicky.

I asked Mia if she remembered a time when she didn't feel this way, and it was then that she remembered the event in the hallway and being bumped by Stacy. She recalled being very concerned that she was going to be put on Stacy's "hit list" and be targeted by her forever after. Even though Stacy never picked on or even acknowledged Mia after that day in the hallway, Mia still carried the fear that Stacy was going to do something to her. Stacy became a lurking tiger in Mia's life, and Mia was waiting for her to jump out at every corner.

We did some tapping together about the event that happened when she was 16, and Mia reported feeling much more relaxed and calm. But she'd spent almost half her life living with a fear and discomfort that something was going to happen to her. Mia was uncomfortable around people and lived life being very guarded. A while after we did the tapping, Mia said that she was able to relax around people and her ability to trust people increased.

This is a big reason that I'm writing this book for you: I don't want you to wait until you're 30 (or even 20) to get relief from the stress that you're carrying around in your backpack. I want you to be able to take charge and feel empowered by addressing these upsets when they happen and not 15 years later.

Had Mia known how to tap when she was 16, she could have gone to the girls' bathroom, closed the door of the stall, and tapped about being bumped in the hallway by Stacy. She could have kept thinking the negative thoughts, but she could have tapped on them. I'll show you how to do this all through the book.

Imagine being in charge of your feelings and taking a few minutes to tap on an emotional upset, almost immediately feeling better, and then going about your enjoyable day. This is what I want for you—the ability to tap on the immediate stuff that happens but also to release the things that have been stored in your backpack. Freedom from a heavy backpack is what awaits you as you read this book and do the exercises.

CASSIDY'S COMMENT

I have everyday stress like getting to school on time, and I've had tolerable stress (I was sick for a while), but as I write this, going into 12th grade, I'm pretty confident that I don't have any toxic stress. I got in the habit of tapping whenever something is bothering me, whether it's big or small. So big, stressful situations bother me less and small situations don't turn into big problems. Please keep reading, learn more about your stress, and then in the next chapter you'll learn how to do the tapping.

How Do You Deal with Stress Now?

As a teenage girl you're dealing with so much on a daily basis and then—if it's a particularly stressful time of year with exams, competitions, or performances—your stress can feel like it's skyrocketing and one more piece of information might just cause an overload.

What are some of the things you do now to help you deal with stress? You might not even realize you're drawn to an activity or exercise because you're stressed. Doing things because you're stressed is different from doing things that help alleviate the stress. This chart shows the difference.

Things you may do because you're stressed	Things you may do to alleviate stress
Bite fingernails	Exercise
Get lost in video games	Play sports
Overeat or undereat	Write in journal
Oversleep	Do creative writing: stories, poetry, lyrics
Yell, get angry	Play music
Act aggressively	Meditate
Lash out at people	Help others
Get grouchy	Tap!

This book will help you notice the things you're doing *because* you're stressed. Someone might have already pointed out the change in your mood or commented on your eating habits. I get that you might already have great methods for alleviating stress—and I want you to add tapping to that list! Just keep reading and tapping along with the exercises in this book and soon you'll find that you're doing fewer of the things you did because you were stressed.

"Why am I stressed but my friend isn't?"

Everybody is unique, so your reaction to things will be totally different from your BFF's. Also, your stress backpack is carrying different events, emotions, and upsets than your friend's. So if you get a C on a math test, that might be a huge relief (for me it would have been a miracle) and you might even feel great about it. But we all know someone who would freak out if she got a C in any subject. That stress goes right into her stress backpack and stays there until her thoughts, feelings, and beliefs about it are resolved.

Not only are your stresses going to be different from your friends'; how you respond to stress will also be different. Probably the biggest reason for this is that even though you think you're exactly alike, the truth is that you think very differently than your friend. And a big part of growing up and maturing is that your own thoughts and feelings become more and more unique to you.

Are you getting a good idea of what stress is and how unique your stress is? Great! And guess what? All your reactions to stress are perfectly normal. Even if your parent, coach, or teacher is telling you to get a grip and stop freaking out, having these reactions is *normal*. So the chances are pretty good that you're a normal teenage girl. I'm using the word *normal* a lot because I want you to see as you go through this book that *it's normal* to have thoughts, feelings, and reactions about events, issues, and challenges you're facing.

"But maybe I really love the drama . . ."

Have you been told that you're addicted to drama, or have you been called a drama queen? Maybe you get a lot of attention when you're caught up in drama, and maybe it feels kind of exciting to be the center of attention. But it takes a lot of energy to be in drama mode all the time. And you have to admit that while it might feel exciting, it is super stressful. What kind of royal stress backpack would a drama queen be carrying around?

When your energy is going into drama mode, you have less energy to deal with the things you want and need to deal with every day. So if you think you might be a drama queen, this book is going to help you get in touch with how you're really thinking and feeling about the events that are dramatic in your life. If you've been used to jumping into drama, you're going to be relieved to learn how to stay calmer.

Don't Rebel and Miss Out on Feeling Better!

Even if you feel a little rebellious while reading this book because somebody has given it to you in hopes that you'll change your behavior, I want you to know that this book is *not* about fixing you (you're not broken) or changing you (you're wonderful the way you are). This book *is* about giving you some simple tools that you can use every day when you feel like your reactions to stress are interfering with your peace, calm, and happiness. Do this for yourself.

. . . .

CASSIDY'S COMMENT

Okay, guys, it's time to learn how to tap. I'm going to be honest with you, it's going to look weird. For real, you're going to be using your fingertips to tap on your face, body, and head. I usually tap in private to avoid strange looks. But it will be worth it. Go somewhere private to read the next bit because you're going to want to try it immediately. The truth is, this tapping thing could be one of the best things you do for yourself in your whole life. It has changed mine.

Chapter 2

. . . .

HOW TO TAP

Have you ever put your face in your hands when something upsetting happens? Or clasped your hand to your chest when you've had a fright? Do you feel soothed if someone is brushing your hair? Without even knowing it, you've experienced touch on what are called *acupuncture meridians*—channels of energy that run throughout your body—and when you do that, you get a mini–relaxation treatment. The point is that you already know you can soothe yourself or someone else with touch. Tapping just gives you a structured and proven way to do it.

I love tapping, and teenage girls I've worked with love tapping because it's super easy to do. You do it the same way every time you want to feel better about something, and with a little practice you really experience the benefits. Lots of girls say that they love it because it's theirs, it's private, and they feel empowered when they take charge of how they're feeling by tapping for a few minutes.

The tapping process has seven easy steps. I'm going to take you through each one in detail, with lots of examples, but first, here's an overview:

1. Choose what you want to tap on—your tapping target topic (what's bugging you?).

2. Rate the level of intensity of the issue on a scale of 0 to 10 (how much is it bugging you?).

3. Create a setup statement that describes your issue, and come up with a reminder phrase.

4. With one hand, tap on a point on the side of your other hand—it's called the karate chop point—while repeating your setup statement out loud three times.

5. Tap gently with your fingertips on the eight EFT points you'll learn about in this chapter, while saying your reminder phrase out loud. You'll tap each point five to seven times.

6. When you've tapped the eight points, take a deep breath and rate the level of intensity of your feeling again to check your progress.

7. You've just completed one tapping round. Repeat the same round until you're feeling better.

It seems easy, right? It is! Now I'll give you all the details you need for each of these seven steps. If you like to see stuff in action and learn by watching, you can see the "How to Tap" video at www.christinewheeler.com/tappingvideo.

. . . .

CASSIDY'S COMMENT

So this part of the book is the most important part for you to read. This is where you're going to learn all about this weird (yes, it's weird) tapping thing that I learned from Chris when I was around seven years old. You're going to see how you can do this super simple exercise that will help calm you when you're upset about something. It really doesn't matter what you're upset about either. I've tapped on pretty much everything that's bothered me since I was seven!

In this chapter, you're going to learn the first part of tapping, which is to figure out what you're upset about and create sentences about it. It's easy and kind of fill-in-the-blank, and Chris will walk you through the whole thing.

Then you'll see a diagram of a person with a bunch of points on the face and body, and you're going to take your fingertips and tap on these specific points. These are like special energy points that send calming information into your body and into your brain, and somehow it works—you feel calmer. I've been so surprised after tapping on big-deal things because they just didn't bother me anymore. I couldn't even get upset about them if I tried. I can't tell you what a relief that is—to be totally freaked out about something (like singing in front of a group or presenting in front of my class) and then tapping and being totally comfortable.

Okay, I know it looks weird to do it, but go in your room or the bathroom and shut the door. Nobody needs to see you do it. Yes, you're tapping on your face and saying stuff that's bugging you. But I'm telling you, sometimes I feel like a wizard when I'm doing this. I feel so powerful that I can take charge of my own feelings and thoughts and feel better almost instantly.

Please try it. It totally works! I promise!

. . . .

Seven Simple Steps

Step 1: Choose your tapping target

Let's start by choosing a topic to tap on. What do you want to target? Is there something that's bugging you right now? Remember how we talked about your stress backpack? There might be something in there that's upsetting, stressful, or annoying. It might be something like this:

- I'm so stressed about school.
- My brother is really annoying me.
- My friend and I had a fight and I can't stop thinking about it.

Here are some good questions to ask yourself to help you pick a tapping target.

- What happened today that's bugging me?
- What's stressful in my life right now?
- What have I stored in my stress backpack?
- What am I worrying about right now?

What do you think? Grab your notebook and take a few moments to answer these questions and you might get quite a list. Or you might not even need to get a list, you might have something that pops right to the surface! Remember, you're just learning tapping right now and this whole book is full of tapping targets. So for now, pick just one thing and write it down. I really encourage you to write it down because it helps you keep track of what you're working on. Keep in mind that there is no wrong answer when you pick an issue to work on. If something is bothering you, then that's your target.

So let's say that your issue is *I'm so stressed about school*. That's pretty general, right? And believe me, I understand that school in general may be stressing you out. And, yes, tapping on general things is likely to help you feel better. But there are so many things going on at school that are much more specific: classes, teachers, friends, activities, exams, report cards.

So if I asked you what specifically was stressing you about school, you might say, "I'm not doing well at math and it's freaking me out." And if I asked you what *feelings* you have about the stress, you might say, "I don't get math sometimes and I feel stupid and frustrated." See how much more specific that is than saying, "I'm so stressed about school"?

Let's break this down again:

- Here's our first, general tapping target: *I'm so stressed about school!*

- Getting more specific with the target: *I'm stressed because I'm not doing well in math.*

- Getting even more specific, adding feelings: *I'm frustrated because I'm not doing well in math and I feel stupid.*

You can use the same process with any issue that is bothering you. Let's look at another one.

- Here's another general tapping target: *My brother is really annoying me.*

- Getting more specific, ask yourself *how* he is annoying you. You might say, *He's trying to hack into my phone to read my texts.*

- Getting even more specific, ask yourself how you feel about his actions. You might say, *I'm so angry that he's invading my privacy and being such a jerk.*

You're getting this, right? As you get more specific, you can see that you're not just annoyed, you're angry about your brother invading your privacy. Your specific tapping target is *I'm so angry at my brother for invading my privacy and being such a jerk.*

Step 2: Measure your level of intensity

How much is it bugging you?

I'd love it if you'd get into the habit of measuring the level of intensity you're feeling about your tapping target and writing it down. This is a way to help you keep track of your progress as you go about the tapping exercises. Another reason I like to have you write it down is because after the tapping is complete, you can often forget how intense it was to start with. I know that sounds wild, but it's true—tapping can be that effective!

What do I mean by "level of intensity"? I mean, how bad is it right now? How awful do you feel? How uncomfortable are you right now? On a scale of 0 to 10, where 0 means that you don't feel any distress at all and 10 is the worst it could be, how would you measure the way you're feeling right now? Look at your tapping target statement: *I'm so angry that my brother's invading my privacy and being such a jerk.* Right now in this moment, how big is your anger on a scale of 0 to 10?

If you're so upset that you feel like you're seething, then you're probably at a 10 out of 10. If you feel a little calmer than you did when you first found your brother snooping on your phone, you might be at a level of intensity of 5 or 6 out of 10. Don't worry about getting this number "right." When you first start paying attention to your issues this way, everything might feel like a 10 out of 10! Or sometimes a number will pop into your head that represents how you're feeling, even if you didn't decide on it consciously. Just write it down.

Step 3: Create your setup statement and reminder phrase

Now that you know the level of intensity you're feeling about your issue, the next step is to create what we call the *setup statement*. The purpose of this statement is to focus your attention and your energy on your tapping target in a deliberate way. The basic setup statement goes like this:

Even though _____ [fill in the blank with your target], I love and accept myself.

Going back to our examples, your setup statement might be *Even though I'm so angry at my jerk brother, I love and accept myself* or *Even though I'm so frustrated that I feel stupid in math, I love and accept myself.* It might sound clunky at first, but that doesn't matter. Keep at it and it'll get easier with some practice.

"Why do I have to say I love and accept myself?"

I know that this part of the setup statement is strange to say for some people and I get that we don't have the habit of saying "I love and accept myself" to ourselves. So it might feel super weird to say this, especially out loud. What we are doing when we say this part of the setup statement is acknowledging that we have this problem or issue, but we have love and compassion for ourselves despite it. We're not mad at ourselves for having the feelings that we have.

Have you ever said to your friend, parent, or sibling that you'd love them no matter what? That's what you'll be saying to yourself with these words while you're tapping. You don't even have to believe it; while you're tapping, the message gets through. But if it feels too weird to use those exact words, try something like:

- Even though _____, I'm still awesome.
- Even though _____, I'm still a good person.
- Even though _____, I'm still cool.
- Even though _____, I still rock.
- Even though _____, I'm okay.
- Even though _____, I love me no matter what.

Or choose your own phrase to end your setup statement. Just make sure it's positive. And then work your way up to actually saying, "I love and accept myself."

What the setup statement is really saying

Do you ever feel like people aren't listening to you when you're trying to talk about a problem that's upsetting you? You want them to know and understand that this is really bothering you: you're really angry that your brother is invading your privacy, or you're frustrated at feeling stupid with math. But it seems like they're just not getting it. Maybe they're not even paying attention.

When you create your setup statement and say *Even though I'm angry that my brother is invading my privacy* . . . you're telling your mind, your body, and your whole being that *you* are listening, and you *are* paying attention. You're reaching into your heart and soul and pulling up this problem you have, and you're saying it out loud, writing it down in your notebook, and being very deliberate in your acknowledgment of the problem. *You are listening to you!* Trust me on this, your brain loves it when it knows you're paying attention!

Craft your reminder phrase

Now that you've got your tapping target and written it down, you'll create a simple phrase that helps you stay focused on this problem while you're tapping the EFT points. Just pick a few words that you'll say out loud while tapping each point.

You might use the word that describes your feeling as well as a word or two to describe what it's about: *frustrated about math* or *I feel stupid about math*. Remember that you can't do this wrong. Another example would be *angry at my jerk brother*.

The fun part of the reminder phrase is that as you get used to tapping, you can change your phrase as you tap each point. This helps you express all the feelings you have about your issue. *I'm so angry at him . . . he's such a jerk . . . I can't even deal . . .* It's very cathartic when you rant and tap at the same time!

Step 4: Tap on the karate chop point

Now that you've crafted your setup statement and your reminder phrase, it's time to try the tapping. This is how you actually send these new signals to your brain.

You start by tapping the fleshy side of one hand with the fingers of your opposite hand. (See the diagram on page 20.) It doesn't matter which hand you tap, and you can switch back and forth. Tap firmly enough that you can feel it, like you were drumming your fingers on the table. You'll find your own rhythm of tapping as you practice.

While constantly tapping this point, say your setup statement out loud three times. I know you're making a face about saying this out loud. I get it, you don't want people to hear what you're saying. But please at least whisper the words if you can't say them out loud. We want the words to really have an impact, and saying them helps your brain to register them more than if you're just reading them and thinking them. Whispering is okay, but if you can say them out loud, please do, and get this: the louder the better! If the thing is bugging you so much that you want to yell, then that's the force you should try to put behind your voice when saying your setup statement. There's a way you can actually sort of yell in a whisper. You might find that you get really good at whisper-yelling!

So, tap on the karate chop point and say your setup statement three times:

Karate Chop: Even though I'm angry that my brother is invading my privacy, I love and accept myself.
Karate Chop: Even though I'm angry that my brother is invading my privacy, I love and accept myself.
Karate Chop: Even though I'm angry that my brother is invading my privacy, I love and accept myself.

Step 5: Tap through the points and repeat the reminder phrase

After repeating your setup statement three times while tapping the karate chop point, it's time to move on to tapping the rest of the EFT points. You can tap points on either side of your body, or both sides if you feel like it. You're tapping on energy points that run down both sides of the body along those meridians I mentioned earlier. Have a look at the diagram of the points below and practice tapping on them right now. Just tapping the points might help you feel a bit calmer, even without adding any words.

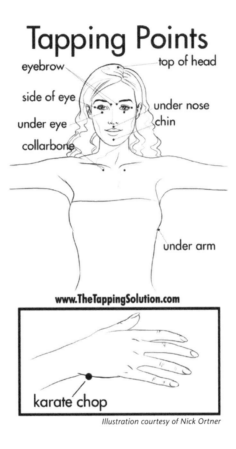

Illustration courtesy of Nick Ortner

As you tap each point, you'll repeat your reminder phrase out loud or in a whisper. You'll take one or two fingers from either hand and tap each of these points five to seven times, or as long as it takes you to repeat your reminder phrase.

Eyebrow: I'm angry that my brother is invading my privacy . . .
Side of Eye: I'm angry that my brother is invading my privacy . . .
Under Eye: I'm angry that my brother is invading my privacy . . .

Under Nose: I'm angry that my brother is invading my privacy . . .

Chin: I'm angry that my brother is invading my privacy . . .

Collarbone: I'm angry that my brother is invading my privacy . . .

Under Arm: I'm angry that my brother is invading my privacy . . .

Top of Head: I'm angry that my brother is invading my privacy . . .

When I suggest tapping five to seven times on each point, that's just a guideline. As you get more and more used to tapping, you might feel like you want to tap a certain point more often than others. If so, do it! As you're learning and practicing, I want you to include all the points, and when you're tapping on a specific target, you should also use all the points. But if something has just happened that's upsetting or bothering you, and it's tough to go through the whole tapping sequence, just tap a point or two and you're likely to get some quick relief until you can find the time and space to tap a full sequence.

• •

CASSIDY'S COMMENT

If something has just happened and I'm somewhere I can't do a full round of tapping, I just tap on the karate chop point and it helps me to feel better right away. It gives me the ability to tap in public, which is great when I am right about to go onstage, get up in front of a class, or whatever it is that I am anxious about. If you have only one hand free, you can tap the karate chop point on that hand against your leg, a table, or any other surface. Try it!

• •

Step 6: Check in

You've just completed one round of tapping! Nice work! Now take a deep breath. Notice how you're feeling. Doing this can take some getting used to, so ask yourself these questions:

1. Did my feelings about this change at all?

2. What thoughts came up while I was tapping?

3. On a scale of 0 to 10, how do I feel about my issue *now*?

Your anger about your brother's nosiness might have shifted from an 8 out of 10 to a 4 out of 10.

Step 7: Repeat the same tapping round until you're feeling even better

Once you get to Step 7, you've completed one round of tapping. Easy, right? Different, right? You've checked in with how you're feeling, and sometimes when you're tapping on a specific issue you might get instant relief. Seriously, you might feel so much better after a single round of tapping that you forget what was bugging you so much. It's not your imagination! An issue, even one you feel really, really bad about, can clear away, neutralize, disappear in one round of tapping.

Or you may find you still have some upset about it. If so, you can do another round of tapping using the same setup statement. Sometimes it takes a couple of rounds of tapping. Sometimes it can take 10 rounds. But the deal is that you have to keep tapping. *I want you to make a promise to yourself* that you'll keep doing rounds of tapping until you feel better about your issue, tapping target, upset—whatever you want to call it. Please keep tapping until your issue is getting harder and harder to be upset about. This may mean that your level of intensity is down to a 2 or 3 out of 10. You may want to continue tapping until you're at a 0, but it's up to you.

This may sound like a lot of work, but remember that once you have your setup statement and reminder phrase prepared, a round of tapping takes a matter of seconds. And what that means is that even with several rounds of tapping, you could feel better in minutes!

The thing about feeling better

Feeling less angry about your nosy brother doesn't mean that it's okay for him to try to hack your phone and read your private texts. It just means that when you think about it, it doesn't cause you as much distress. *Tapping is all about helping YOU feel better.* When you're feeling a bit calmer about something, it's often easier to find solutions to address the problem. You may even be able to speak to your parents more calmly about how you feel about his invasion of your privacy.

Tapping Quick Reference Guide

1. Choose a topic/target/issue.

2. Rate the level of intensity of your chosen issue on a scale of 0 to 10.

3. Create a setup statement that describes your issue and come up with a simple reminder phrase.

4. Tap on the karate chop point while repeating the setup statement three times.

5. Tap gently using your fingertips on the eight EFT points while saying your reminder phrase out loud. You'll tap each point five to seven times.

6. Check in. When you've tapped the eight points, take a deep breath and rate your level of intensity again on a scale of 0 to 10 to check your progress.

7. Repeat the same sequence or tapping round until you're feeling better about your issue.

Moving Targets: Tapping through the Layers

While you're tapping on one issue, you might find that thoughts come up about something else. For example, while you're tapping on the anger about your little brother's nosiness, you might have the thought that your parents haven't been paying attention to your complaints about him, and you might be angry about this too.

It's the same emotion (anger), but it's directed at others (parents). Your anger at your brother has subsided to maybe a 2 out of 10, but the anger at your parents might be an 8 out of 10. The way I look at it is that underneath the anger at your brother is anger at your parents.

I don't know why issues get stored in layers this way, but think of it as stuff in your stress backpack. You pull out a couple of things and tap on them and then when you look inside again, there's something you didn't know was stuck in there, weighing you down.

If that's the case, then you can make the new issue a tapping target of its own, with a new setup statement, something like *Even though I'm angry that my parents aren't taking this seriously, I love and accept myself.* Your reminder phrase could be *angry at my parents.* But put this new target aside and save it until you've finished working with the tapping target you started with.

It's always a good idea to have your notebook ready so you can write things like this down. You might even have a section in your notebook labeled "Stuff to Tap on Later"! I did that myself and sometimes I would go to that section and I already felt better about the things I'd planned to tap on. This happens a lot because as we feel calmer about one thing that was upsetting, it's like the calmness spreads to other areas of our lives. It's pretty cool.

. . . .

CASSIDY'S COMMENT

Maybe you like having these seven steps of tapping to follow and fillingin the blanks to create your setup statement and reminder phrase. That's great and it's an awesome way to practice tapping and get used to it.

You might want to mix things up, though, and be more creative with the setup phrases and the reminder phrases. I always play with the wording when I tap at home.

For example, saying the same sentence over and over again can get kind of boring, so instead of repeating the same setup statement three times, you could switch it up but stay on the same topic.

Karate Chop: Even though I'm worried about school, I love and accept myself.
Karate Chop: Even though I'm not getting science, I love and accept myself.
Karate Chop: Even though I'm not liking science, I'd like to have science wizard powers.

Then you can play around with the reminder phrase like this:

Eyebrow: I'm worried about school . . .
Side of Eye: Well, it's just science, really . . .
Under Eye: I'm not getting science right now . . .
Under Nose: I don't like science . . .
Chin: I don't like my teacher . . .
Collarbone: I'd rather feel more relaxed . . .
Under Arm: I'd like to be a science wizard . . .
Top of Head: I'm going to be calmer about science.

When I've been tapping and I'm feeling better about the issue, I like changing the wording so that it's more positive and empowering. It's a fun way to acknowledge and tap into how I'd rather be feeling about the issue!

As you get more and more comfortable with tapping, feel free to play around with the wording. This whole book is full of examples of how to do that.

Stealth Tapping

What if you're in a stressful situation where tapping could really help, but there are lots of people around and you feel self-conscious? While tapping isn't anything to be embarrassed about, it's understandable that you might not want a whole bunch of people to watch you tapping on your head and start asking you what you're doing. That might just raise your stress instead of reducing it! So I'm going to give you some tips for tapping under the radar.

Cassidy's already shared one with you on page 21: try just tapping on the karate chop point. No one will notice, but you'll feel better! Another option is to do a full round of tapping using energy meridian points on your *fingertips* instead of on your face, head, and body. We practitioners don't use these finger points as much as we used to in the early years of EFT, but I find them really useful because they're easier to use on their own, when you want to tap but you're not in a place where there's privacy to tap on the main tapping points.

Put your hand out in front of you with your palm facing down so that your thumb is nearest your body. We're going to find the tapping points. Have a look at the picture below.

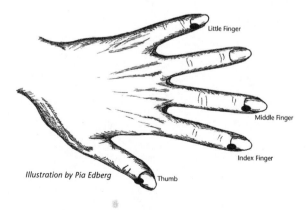

Little Finger

Middle Finger

Index Finger

Illustration by Pia Edberg Thumb

- The **thumb** point is at the base of the nail bed on the side of the thumb closest to you.

- The **index finger** point is at the base of the nail bed on the side of the index finger closest to you.

- The **middle finger** point is at the base of the nail bed on the side of the middle finger closest to you.

- The **little finger** point is at the base of the nail bed on the side of the little finger closest to you.

  Another great technique for stealth tapping is the Butterfly Hug. You can do this anytime, anywhere:

- Cross your arms as if you were giving yourself a hug.

- Put the palm of your left hand on your right upper arm.

- Put the palm of your right hand on your left upper arm.

- Now tap your palms on your upper arms, alternating left, right, left, right.

- Get a comfortable rhythm going and tap this way for 30 seconds or so.

- While tapping this way, notice any feelings of anxiety, upset, or discomfort.

- Keep tapping until you feel calmer.

When to Tap

Quick tapping breaks for practice

Anytime you have a few minutes, like when you're taking a shower or using the bathroom, please play with tapping on the eight points. Don't worry about the setup statement and reminder phrase; just focus on getting used to tapping on the points! Practicing this is the way to make tapping an instant stress-relief habit. When you feel like tapping the points is as familiar as snapping your fingers, then begin adding a setup statement and reminder phrase during these quick tapping breaks.

Tap in the moment!

As soon as something happens that's upsetting, start tapping! I want you to start practicing all the tapping points now so the habit is there and can become an automatic response when something happens. You might not have the privacy to tap a full round, but remember the karate chop and the fingertip tapping points and use those whenever you can. If you're at school when something happens to upset you, take a bathroom break and tap.

Homework tapping

A great time to tap is just before sitting down to do your homework. Take a five-minute tapping break and tap on the things that bothered you during the day. If you feel aggravated because you have to do homework, tap on that. This way you clear your mind and feel calmer as you approach your homework.

Empty your backpack at bedtime

One of my favorite things for you to try is to tap before you go to bed. If you keep a journal and you write about your day and the good things and the not-so-good things that happened, take a few extra minutes and tap on it all. Even if you don't write down your daily experiences, tap about them.

Tap on the things that happened that bothered you that day. You can do a whole setup statement and round of tapping with reminder phrases, or just tap the points while talking to yourself quietly about the things that bothered you. Then do one round of tapping on the points while thinking about things that went *well* that day. Maybe you did well on a test, or you had a chat with someone you like. If you're still awake after this, you can also tap on the great things you want to do tomorrow.

If you empty your backpack at the end of the day by tapping on the things that bothered you, you'll have a more peaceful sleep and you'll wake up the next day with a clearer mind.

Tap while listening to music or watching movies

For many of us, music and lyrics can evoke strong emotions. What are some songs that make you cry? I know that it can feel awesome and cathartic to cry your eyes out while listening to your favorite heart-wrenching music. Add tapping to that and you'll feel even better! Do you always cry at commercials on TV, or when you're watching movies? That's normal and it means that you have emotion sitting on the surface that wants to be expressed. Tap while you're watching a movie and see what happens. Don't worry about setup statements—just tap.

Remembering to tap

Please add tapping to your daily life. Play with tapping until it becomes as routine as brushing your teeth. (In fact, while you're brushing your teeth, try tapping the points with your other hand!) I want you to tap so that when something upsetting happens, tapping is the first thing that comes to mind.

When I was first learning to tap, I'd place sticky notes everywhere as a reminder to tap. You can put a pop-up reminder on your phone or add it to your calendar. Make it fun, leave yourself notes:

If you feel like crap, then tap
If you want to be napping, then you could be tapping

The more you use tapping to get relief as soon as an upset happens, the more quickly you'll bounce back from it. You don't have to let an upset take over and undermine your confidence, your sense of self, or your happiness. Be resilient by using tapping as soon as something happens.

Helping your family and friends

Once you've been doing the tapping exercises in the book for a while, your friends and family are likely to notice that you're calmer, more peaceful, and happier. When they ask you why you're so unstressed and awesome even though exams are happening, that's a good time to tell them about tapping. But remember that some people won't care how enthusiastic you are about tapping, they will just think it's weird. That's okay—it's not up to you to get everyone on board.

Keep up with your own tapping and try it out on different things. One day a friend might ask if you've ever tried your weird tapping things for cramps. You'll say how great it worked for you and show her how to do it.

Tapping with study buddies or team members

If you're getting together with your friends to study for an exam or work on a school project together, think about getting everybody tapping. First make sure you feel comfortable introducing this to your friends. It's also fun to notice how well everyone did on the exam after tapping. Imagine your study group getting the highest grades in class!

If it feels comfortable, I totally recommend tapping with your teammates or fellow performers before a game, a swim meet, or a performance. If your gymnast friend is having trouble nailing her landing, show her tapping. You know how to create setup statements and reminder phrases like *Even though I can't nail the landing, I love and accept myself.*

Tapping when you're ranting with your friends

You know how sometimes it can feel so satisfying to tell your best friend every detail of what someone said or did, and how when you're doing that together you both get more and more upset and intense? I know it's fun to commiserate and complain and get into the drama, but does it really resolve anything? Probably not. Instead it probably creates grudges and bad feelings toward the person you're complaining about.

So, what if you tap while you're telling the story to your friend or a group of friends? What if everyone taps together while you're telling your story?

. . . .

CASSIDY'S COMMENT

This is such a great tip. You know how you get so upset about something that, as soon as you start talking about it, it turns into a giant rant and you wind up getting even more upset? But if you tap on all the points you're learning in the next few pages while you're ranting, you will feel calmer. I love it because I instantly feel better and I'm not stuck with being upset for the rest of the day. So if something happens at school and my mom is driving me home, I'll rant and tap and by the time we're home, I feel better and I actually forget about what happened because it's just not a big deal anymore.

. . . .

Chapter 3

WHAT CAN I TAP ON?

Now that you know how to tap, what can you tap on?

The short answer is that you can tap on anything that's bugging you. Seriously. Imagine anything that's bugged you in the last few days.

- Even though my BFF sent me a nasty text, I love and accept myself.
- Even though I skinned my knee playing soccer, I'm still awesome.
- Even though I'm getting a cold, I rock.
- Even though I'm super sleepy but I have to study, I love and accept myself.

You get it, right? The basic rule is that you can tap on anything. You might say, "What about X?" Yes, you can tap on that too. If you're upset about something, don't hesitate—just start tapping. To be more specific, here's the breakdown: you can tap on *events*, you can tap on *thoughts*, you can tap on *feelings*, and you can tap on *actions*.

You Can Tap on Events

What just happened? Was it upsetting? That's an event that you can tap on. Remember Mia from Chapter 1, who was bumped in the hallway? The bump in the hallway was the event. If Mia had tapped on that event right away, she wouldn't have spent her lunch hour obsessing about it and waiting for something awful to happen.

She could have simply tapped: *Even though Stacy just bumped me in the hallway, I love and accept myself.*

The fact is, events happen. Some are positive and some are negative:

- Your parents won't let you go to a movie
- Your friend says something funny
- Your brother reads your texts
- You get an A on a test
- You get a C on a test
- You get a part in the school play
- You don't get picked for the team
- You come in first in the competition
- The person you like ignores you
- The teacher hands out a pop quiz
- You get called on in class
- You get startled by something
- You fall and skin your knee
- Your pet dies
- The person you like flirts with you

Any event that's negative, and therefore upsetting, is something to tap on, and it's super easy to create a setup phrase from anything on this list.

Karate Chop: Even though the person I like ignored me, I'm still awesome.
Karate Chop: Even though I got a C on that test, I love and accept myself.
Karate Chop: Even though I got called on in class, I love and accept myself.

Sometimes even positive events can feel pretty unnerving. Maybe they leave you feeling wound up, overexcited, or worried about what's going to happen next. You can tap on these events as well.

Karate Chop: Even though the person I like flirted with me, I love and accept myself.

Karate Chop: Even though I came in first in the competition, I love and accept myself.
Karate Chop: Even though I got that part in the play, I am awesome.

I know the wording of these setup statements sounds clunky and weird because it seems like we're saying, "Even though I'm excited and happy, I love and accept myself"—as if being excited and happy is a bad thing. Remember earlier I said that even good stress is stressful? Here, we're acknowledging that the excited feeling is causing some stress and we want to calm that stress so we can feel calmer and rock the next steps.

You can tap on past events

Is there an event from your past that you never really got over? Something you still think about, that's still upsetting you even though it happened months or years ago? Maybe people are telling you that you need to get over it, move on, and stop sulking about it. But it's difficult, right? It can feel like you're stuck there. Tapping will help you unstick these past events.

Here are some examples of past events that might keep you stuck.

Past Event
Something Happened
My parents got divorced
My grandparent died
I broke up with my person
I had an illness
My BFF moved away

Any of these events is a great tapping target, and you can see how easily you can create your setup statements and begin tapping right away.

Karate Chop: Even though my parents divorced, I love and accept myself.
Karate Chop: Even though my grandparent died, I love and accept myself.

When you're tapping on past events, you still check in with your level of intensity on a scale of 0 to 10. But you check in with how you're feeling *now*, not how you felt when it first happened. Make sense? So when your BFF moved away, that might have felt like a 20 out of 10. Now time has passed, so you measure how upset you feel about it now.

Make your own list of events from the past that still bother you, that you feel like you never quite got over. You might fill in the blank:

I haven't been the same since _____ *happened.*

Some girls give themselves a tapping spa treatment once a week and set aside 10 or 15 minutes to tap on past events from their lists. The timing is up to you; some girls do this before bed and others pick a weekend afternoon. Anytime is a good time to tap on these past events and get back on track to being your awesome self.

You can tap on present events

Remember earlier I asked you to practice tapping the points so you get used to using them and it becomes a habit? I want you to have this habit locked in so that when something happens that bugs you, you can start tapping right away. Tap as soon as you can. If possible, try to tap while the event is still happening.

Imagine you're sitting in class and you're watching presentations and you know you're up next. As you watch your classmate give his speech, you start feeling nervous. At your desk, while you're waiting, tap on your finger points the way I showed you in Chapter 2.

Present Event
Something's Happening
I have a pop quiz
I fall and skin my knee
I'm in a fight with my friend
I have a performance/game

Tapping on present events is an awesome way to deal more calmly with something that's happening right now. If you've just been surprised by a pop quiz and you tap away at your finger points for a couple of minutes, you'll clear your mind and activate your brain's ability to focus. I get that you're not going to do a round of tapping out loud, with a setup statement and reminder phrases, while sitting in class! Tapping silently is a great alternative to staring at the page and sweating because you didn't do your homework the night before.

. . . .

CASSIDY'S COMMENT

I love this so much! I use the finger points or the karate chop point on the side of my hand and tap when I'm about to take an exam. It takes my nervousness and worry right away and helps me focus. When the teacher hands out the exam, I can jump into it with confidence and a calm mind. It has honestly saved my life.

. . . .

You can tap on future events

One of the best uses of tapping is to calm the anticipation you might have about future events.

Future Event
Something's Going to Happen
I have finals coming up
I have the lead in the school play
My team is going to the playoffs

Imagine being able to calm your nervousness and anxiety about an upcoming event, whether it's an exam, performance, game, or competition. You know how you can feel clammy and get a knot in your stomach just thinking about a future event like one of these? Tapping now about something that's going to happen can help you prepare calmly. Whether you're studying, practicing, researching, or just thinking about the future event, tapping will help you do all those things with more ease and confidence. So if you ever find yourself saying that you're dreading that soccer game, school play, or exam, take the time to tap now. You might even calm yourself enough to notice that you're actually excited!

You Can Tap on Your Thoughts

Kinds of thoughts: helpful, neutral, and unhelpful

There are three kinds of thinking: helpful, neutral, and unhelpful thinking. You already know what you want to shoot for, right?

Helpful thinking is happening when you're doing your best problem solving. You're moving in a positive direction in your thoughts and coming up with some great ideas. Unhelpful thinking doesn't move you in a positive direction and it doesn't feel good. It can seem like you're getting caught in a loop of thought without coming to a solution. I think of it sometimes like getting stuck on a hamster wheel . . . the hamster wheel of doom. Neutral thinking, meanwhile, is just what it sounds like: neither negative nor positive. Tapping helps remind your mind that being neutral feels better than thinking unhelpful thoughts and can help ease your way toward more helpful ones.

Remember Mia?

Remember Mia and her 14 thoughts about being bumped in the hallway by Stacy? You can check those thoughts out again on page 5 if you want to. Do you think Mia's thinking was helpful or unhelpful? Her first two thoughts were actually pretty neutral: *That was so weird* and *She seems upset, I wonder if she's okay.* But you can see that it didn't take long to go from *That was so weird* to *OMG!* and *Why does stuff like this always happen to me?*

We're not judging Mia's thoughts, but her thoughts about the event in the hallway were definitely unhelpful. As they escalated, they became more and more negative. You can tell how unhelpful they were because that event stuck with her for 14 years.

It's pretty easy to tell if your thoughts are helpful or unhelpful. Here are a few characteristics of unhelpful thoughts:

- They tend to be negative.
- They don't move you forward toward resolution or problem solving.

- They can be self-critical—*I'm such an idiot* or *It's all my fault.*
- They can be worst-case scenarios—*My parents are going to kill me.*
- They can be catastrophizing—*I will never get over this.*
- They can overgeneralize—*Everyone is mad at me.*
- They can involve mind reading—*I know they hate me and they think I'm ugly.*
- They can be judgmental—*She is such a loser.*
- They can be comparing—*She's so much prettier/smarter/taller/ better than me.*

Do you recognize any familiar ways of thinking when you read this? What kind of unhelpful thoughts have you been thinking? Don't be hard on yourself about it (that's unhelpful thinking), but do pay attention to the content of your thoughts. When you do, you can start to change that content from unhelpful to neutral and even helpful. And tapping is an awesome way to do this!

What do you think?

How do you start paying attention to your thoughts? Get out your notebook if you haven't done so already. I want you to write down the kinds of thoughts you notice yourself having. Remember, so much of our thinking is automatic. We look at a thing and we have automatic thoughts about it. We see a girl walking down the street and have an automatic thought about her.

As weird as it sounds, I want you to listen to yourself. Listen to your thoughts, or look at your thoughts as you write them down.

Doing this exercise will help you identify the kinds of thoughts you're thinking. I know it's kind of weird to actually think about what you're thinking! But it's pretty cool that we can do that. Have you ever tried it before? Your thoughts are going to be pretty random, so try not to judge them, just write them down. Try this now for about a minute. Write down as many random thoughts as you can.

Emily was awesome but she battled negative thinking

To the outside world, Emily had everything going for her. She was kind, talented, funny, and smart. She did well in school, people liked her, and she was involved in a number of activities that she loved. But Emily would tell you that her inside world was a mess. Her thoughts were negative, and she would sometimes spiral into thinking the worst was going to happen. She was hard on herself and spoke harshly to herself and, although she was very kind to others, she was very unkind to herself. She felt like she was wearing glasses that filtered out all the good in the world, especially the good in her. She thought she had many failings, and though she was striving to be a good person, she was so critical of herself that she never saw the good in herself, especially when she compared herself to others. She was stressed all the time and on a scale of 0 to 10 she was at a 9. You can see that most of Emily's stress was because of her unhelpful thinking.

When Emily did the exercise in noticing and writing down her thoughts, here's a sample of what she came up with:

- I can't believe I only got a B in science.
- God, you're so stupid.
- Why did you do that?
- She's so pretty.
- She's prettier than me.
- I'm excited about prom.
- What if nobody asks me?

You can see that not every single one of Emily's thoughts was negative. She had a positive thought about prom. But it was immediately followed by a negative, worried thought that she might not be asked to prom.

What do you notice about the thoughts you wrote down? Are there any patterns, like Emily's shift from positive to negative? I know it might be surprising to look at your thoughts on paper, but I want you to be aware of what your own thinking habits are. Then you can use tapping to feel better and to have better thoughts about yourself and others. As you do the tapping exercises in this book, you will find that you're having more and more neutral, and even positive, helpful thoughts about yourself.

Putting events and thoughts together

When an event happens, you have a thought about it instantly. You might not always be aware of your thought, but I guarantee you have one. Have a look at this chart that shows how events and thoughts can go together.

Event	Thought
Something happens	You have a thought
My parents won't let me go to a movie	They never let me do anything
My friend says something funny	That is so hilarious
My brother reads my texts	I can't get any privacy around here
I get an A on a test	I am a super genius
I get a C on a test	I'll never understand physics
I get a part in the school play	OMG, I made it!
I don't get picked for the team	OMG, I'm such a crappy athlete
I come in first in the competition	All that hard work paid off!
The person I like ignores me	They can never like me
The teacher hands out a pop quiz	I shouldn't have watched that movie last night
I get called on in class	Now everyone's looking at me
I get startled by something	I'm in danger

You get that you can tap on an event that's bothering you. Tapping on the event itself is quite general, and though you're likely to feel better, it's just one aspect of your upset. Now you know how to tap on the thoughts you're thinking, which is another aspect of your upset. When you put those together, you can tap on what you're thinking about the event, which is like a double tapping whammy. By covering these two aspects of what's happening, you're likely to get relief even more quickly than if you tapped on one or the other.

You Can Tap on Your Feelings

Feelings are your emotional reaction to the thoughts you have. Maybe it's not 100 percent obvious to you what the difference is. So a great way to get clear about what's a thought and what's a feeling is to fill in the blank in this phrase:

When I think about _____, I feel _____.

For example:

When I think about college, I feel scared.
When I think about prom, I feel excited.
When I think about that person I like, I feel nervous.

When we look at feelings this way, we acknowledge that the mere thought of an event can ignite an uncomfortable feeling. The feeling is another part, or aspect, of the upset. You're not physically in the exam room, taking the exam, but when you think about it, you can have an emotional reaction, a feeling of nervousness. If that emotional reaction feels uncomfortable, then you can use tapping to feel more comfortable about the emotion you're experiencing. Even if it is a good feeling, like excitement, it can be helpful to tap on it, especially if the excitement is keeping you awake, distracting you from your homework, and so on.

"What am I feeling?"

Feelings are pretty complex. And in many societies and cultures, girls are supposed to be nice and polite, and so we may have been taught that it's not acceptable, for example, for us to be angry. We may get confused about what we are really feeling, especially if an adult is telling us that we shouldn't feel angry about something and that it's impolite to express anger. So what happens to your anger? I think it creates stress and gets stuffed into your stress backpack until you take it out and tap on it.

Here's a great list to help you identify what you're feeling when you think about something that just happened that's affecting you, either negatively or positively. I want you to spend some time reading the words that describe feelings and put a mark beside any that might apply to you, or write them in your notebook.

Alone	Discouraged	Inspired	Repulsed
Angry	Dissatisfied	Interested	Resentful
Annoyed	Disturbed	Irritated	Sad
Anxious	Doubtful	Jealous	Satisfied
Apathetic	Enraged	Joyful	Scared
Ashamed	Embarrassed	Mad	Secure
Bold	Enthusiastic	Miserable	Self-conscious
Brave	Euphoric	Nervous	Sensitive
Calm	Excited	Optimistic	Shy
Cheerful	Free	Panicky	Tense
Comfortable	Frightened	Pathetic	Tired
Confused	Frustrated	Peaceful	Thankful
Content	Guarded	Playful	Torn
Curious	Guilty	Pessimistic	Unhappy
Defeated	Happy	Powerful	Uneasy
Depressed	Impatient	Powerless	Unprepared
Detached	Important	Prepared	Upset
Determined	Inferior	Quiet	Vulnerable
Disconnected	Insecure	Relaxed	Worried

Your feelings are your own

Please don't compare your unique feelings with anybody else's feelings. You may feel sad about an event that happened, but your BFF might feel angry about the same event. Your feelings are your own, and when you're having strong feelings that are causing you distress and distracting you from going about your business of being awesome, you can go ahead and tap on those feelings.

Now, this is important: tapping on your feelings will not make you into an emotionless robot. It *will* help you feel less challenged by your feelings. Sometimes feelings can be pretty intense. We want you to feel comfortable, and tapping will help you with that.

Putting events, thoughts, and feelings together

Let's go back to the chart we created that showed how events lead to thoughts. When we add feelings to our chart, we see how complex a reaction to an event really is. What's interesting is that your *feeling* is a reaction to your *thought* about the *event*. So if you find that you have lots of negative, unhelpful thoughts about events that happen, you might also find that your feelings tend to be negative. Any part of the reaction is a great place to start tapping! And tapping on all parts of the reaction can help you feel better about the whole complex thing.

Event	Thought	Feeling
Something happens	You have a thought	That creates a feeling
My parents won't let me go to a movie	They never let me do anything	I feel frustrated
My friend says something funny	That is so hilarious	I feel happy
My brother reads my texts	I can't get any privacy around here!	I feel so angry
I get an A on a test	I am a super genius	I feel proud of myself
I get a C on a test	I'll never understand physics	I feel pessimistic
I get a part in the school play	OMG, I made it!	I feel excited
I don't get picked for the team	OMG, I'm such a crappy athlete	I feel inferior
I come in first in the competition	All that hard work paid off!	I feel euphoric
The person I like ignores me	They can never like me	I feel insecure
The teacher hands out a pop quiz	I shouldn't have watched that movie last night	I feel panicky
I get called on in class	Now everyone's looking at me	I feel embarrassed, uneasy
I get startled by something	I'm in danger	I feel frightened

You Can Tap on Actions

Something happens and you react

Here's how your reaction to an event might seem to work. When something happens you notice it, and then you react with an action. Your action might be to do something like yell, stomp, cry, laugh, and sometimes, your body will have a reaction like wanting to barf, getting butterflies, or your heart starting to race. Here are some examples.

Event	Action
Something Happens	You Do Something
My parents won't let me go to a movie	I stomp out of the room
My friend says something funny	I burst out laughing
My brother reads my texts	I yell at my brother
I get an A on a test	I yell, "Woohoo!"

You get it, right? Something happens and you react! Sometimes your reaction is a physical action and sometimes you feel it in your body. It happens in an instant—but we've already talked about the steps that happen in between, so quickly that you don't even know they're happening. When an *event* happens, you have a *thought* and then you have a *feeling* and then you react with an *action*. Check out our chart now:

Event	Thought	Feeling	Action
Something happens	You have a thought	That creates a feeling	You do something
My parents won't let me go to a movie	They never let me do anything	I feel frustrated	I stomp out of the room
My friend says something funny	That is so hilarious	I feel happy	I burst out laughing
My brother reads my texts	I can't get any privacy around here!	I feel so angry	I yell at my brother
I get an A on a test	I am a super genius	I feel proud of myself	I yell, "Woohoo!"
I get a C on a test	I'll never understand physics	I feel pessimistic	I get a stomachache
I get a part in the school play	OMG, I made it!	I feel excited	I get butterflies in my stomach
I don't get picked for the team	OMG, I'm such a crappy athlete	I feel inferior	I burst into tears
I come in first in the competition	All that hard work paid off!	I feel euphoric	I jump up and down
The person I like ignores me	They can never like me	I feel insecure	I withdraw
The teacher hands out a pop quiz	I shouldn't have watched that movie last night	I feel panicky	I want to barf
I get called on in class	Now everyone's looking at me	I feel embarrassed, uneasy	My stomach churns, my hands sweat, and I have a lump in my throat
I get startled by something	I'm in danger	I feel frightened	I punch, run, freeze, shout

Putting It All Together

You already know human beings are complex and incredible creatures. Isn't it cool to see how you can explore your thoughts and feelings and actions and get to know your awesome self even better? And now you get to take charge and tap on everything that you want to feel better about.

I'm going to show you how to use my method to create your own tapping exercises so you can not only get relief about an event that's upset you, but also calm and neutralize your thoughts, feelings, and reactions to what happened.

Let's take one line from the Event-Thought-Feeling-Action chart and create four different, but connected, tapping targets and setup statements. This perfectly solves the dilemma that lots of people have about trying to decide what to tap on, what words to use, and how to create setup statements. Let's imagine that this is something that's happened for you—and it probably has: I bet you can think of something that you wanted to do but your parents wouldn't let you.

Event	Thought	Feeling	Action
Something happens	You have a thought	That creates a feeling	You do something
My parents won't let me go to a movie	They never let me do anything	I feel frustrated	I stomp out of the room
Tapping Target #1	Tapping Target #2	Tapping Target #3	Tapping Target #4
Reminder Phrase #1	Reminder Phrase #2	Reminder Phrase #3	Reminder Phrase #4

Now, we're going to apply the seven steps of tapping.

Step 1. Pick your tapping target

When you fill in this Event-Thought-Feeling-Action chart, you'll actually have four tapping targets based on the same issue, which gives you lots of tapping options.

- My parents won't let me go to a movie

- They never let me do anything

- I feel frustrated

- I stomp out of the room

Step 2. Rate your level of intensity for each

What's your level of intensity on a scale of 0 to 10 for each of the tapping targets? Write down your numbers, but don't worry about getting them exactly right. You might have a different level of intensity for each of the tapping targets.

- My parents won't let me go to a movie (6 out of 10)

- They never let me do anything (10 out of 10)

- I feel frustrated (8 out of 10)

- I stomp out of the room (5 out of 10)

Step 3. Create a setup statement and a reminder phrase for each

Now you create four setup statements and reminder phrases, one for each tapping target.

Event
Karate Chop: Even though my parents won't let me go to the movie, I love and accept myself.
Reminder phrase: They won't let me go to the movie.

Thought
Karate Chop: Even though they never let me do anything, I love and accept myself.
Reminder phrase: They never let me do anything.

Feeling
Karate Chop: Even though I feel frustrated, I love and accept myself.
Reminder phrase: I feel so frustrated.

Action

> **Karate Chop:** Even though all I can do is stomp out of the room, I love and accept myself.
>
> Reminder phrase: I just stomp out of the room

Step 4. Tap on karate chop point and repeat setup statement.

It's up to you how you want to do this part. You can start with the first setup statement and repeat it three times while tapping the karate chop point. Or you can repeat each of the four setup statements while tapping the karate chop point. You might also start with the setup statement that has the highest level of intensity for you.

Step 5. Tap points while repeating reminder phrases.

You can repeat one reminder phrase over and over while tapping the points or include them all as I've done here.

Eyebrow:	My parents won't let me go to a movie . . .
Side of Eye:	They never let me do anything . . .
Under Eye:	I feel frustrated . . .
Under Nose:	So I stomp out of the room . . .
Chin:	I don't know what else to do . . .
Collarbone:	They never let me do anything . . .
Under Arm:	I feel so frustrated . . .
Top of Head:	I can't believe they won't let me go!

Tap on this round until you feel better. When you're feeling better, meaning your level of intensity is lower, like at a 2 or 3 out of 10, you can add some neutral and positive reminder phrases. Remember that as you're feeling better, you can make your reminder phrases more fun, more creative, and more positive.

Eyebrow:	Well, I did get to go to that concert last week . . .
Side of Eye:	But I really wanted to go to this movie . . .
Under Eye:	I guess they let me do some stuff . . .
Under Nose:	I'd rather not stomp out of the room . . .
Chin:	I'd rather be calmer . . . (neutral)

Collarbone: When I don't get my way . . .
Under Arm: Then maybe I'll get my way more often . . . (positive)
Top of Head: I'm going to be calmer . . .
Eyebrow: I'm going to be calmer . . .

Side of Eye: When I don't get my way . . .
Under Eye: I love getting my way . . .
Under Nose: It makes me happy . . .
Chin: To get what I want . . .
Collarbone: I look forward to getting my way . . .
Under Arm: More and more often . . .
Top of Head: I love getting my way.

Steps 6 and 7: Check in and repeat.

You can see how much better you'll probably be feeling after tapping on things this way, right? It might take a few rounds of tapping on the negative issue or problem, so be easy on yourself and be patient. Keep tapping until you're feeling better! I get it—I'm the queen of impatience. I want things to happen now. But when I feel impatient, I feel stressed, so I still have to do some tapping on patience. Be kind to yourself and don't add to your stress!

Create your own chart

When an upsetting event happens and it messes up your world and you're having a hard time getting over it, create a chart like this. Even if your parents are telling you that you should just be able to get over it, that it's not that big a deal, putting stuff on this chart helps you see why you're having a hard time dealing with this event. You aren't judging your events, thoughts, feelings, and actions, you're looking at them differently and in more detail than you've looked at them before. You want to notice what you're thinking about something and how that affects how you feel and the action you take. When something happens that affects your happiness and your well-being, it is affecting your whole self!

I'm going to say that again, a different way. When something happens to upset you, the fact is, you are upset! Sure, parents, teachers, adults, siblings can say stuff that they think is helpful, like:

- That shouldn't bother you.
- It's not the end of the world.
- It's time to get over that.
- Dust yourself off and move on.
- Why are you so upset about this?
- What's wrong with you?
- Stop whining about it.

The reason they're saying these things to you is because they're different from you. They have different ways of thinking, feeling, processing, and experiencing life and its events. Nobody really knows what you think or how you feel about your event because they are not you. But the tools I'm sharing with you can help you figure out what you feel and think about your event and use tapping to move past it and feel better.

· ·

CASSIDY'S COMMENT

You've done a really great job putting all this together. How does it feel to have this new control over your inner workings? When someone asks you why you had such a strong reaction to something, you know that it's because you had a thought and a feeling in response to an event. Now you'll find it super easy to feel better about whatever is bugging you.

· ·

Please keep on reading, because everything in this book, and anything you ever want to tap on in your life, will have an event, a thought, a feeling, or an action—or more than one of these—at its root. In the chapters ahead, from time to time we'll come back to this chart to help you see how events, thoughts, feelings, and actions can be related around the topic we're discussing. Other times I'll put together setup statements for you so you can jump right into tapping on the topic. You'll breeze through it and find awesome ways to feel better about the things that are bugging you.

Here's your first Tapfirmation to help you keep being awesome! Remember, you can use this phrase to reinforce what you've done in this chapter. Tap on the tapping points or the finger points, or do the Butterfly Hug, while you say this phrase over and over.

TAPFIRMATION

That happened, it's over, and right now I'm okay.

part two

TAPPING ON HOW YOU LOOK AND FEEL

. . . .

CASSIDY'S COMMENT

Okay, we're really getting into it now! It's time to start feeling better about your health inside and out. I'm talking about everything you can imagine, from how you feel about your body, your appearance, and your time of the month to what's going on in your mind. And you can tap on mental health stuff like anxiety, fear, and grief.

So Chris is going to show you some really easy tapping solutions that will help you (if you do the exercises!) feel better about physical and mental health topics. Remember, nobody needs to know you're tapping on this stuff. Go somewhere private, get out your notebook, and start tapping!

. . . .

Chapter 4

TAPPING ABOUT YOUR BODY
AND YOUR APPEARANCE

We already know that events, thoughts, feelings, and actions can create stress that might be affecting your body and your health. In a study done by the American Psychological Association called The Stress in America survey, teenage girls were found to have high levels of stress about their appearance and their bodies. So I'm excited to give you some tools to help you reduce your stress in this area. Your body is yours and it's going to be with you for your whole life. But if you're feeling stressed and thinking unhelpful stuff about your body, then you're having a stressful relationship with your body. Let's see how we can use tapping to get you treating your body like a friend instead of a frenemy.

How do you speak to your changing body?

During the summer before ninth grade, Taylor had a growth spurt. Not only did she get taller, but her breasts grew noticeably. She was still getting used to her new body and dreading going back to school. She had already had comments from boys in her neighborhood that made her really uncomfortable, and although she thought she looked good, she hated the unwanted attention.

Her first week back at school was interesting, with plenty of people doing a double take when she passed them in the hallway. Most people said she looked beautiful and only a few people made creepy comments, so she was breathing a sigh of relief. That is, until PE class.

That morning she was in a rush and forgot to wear her new sports bra for extra support, so running around in PE was physically uncomfortable. Then she noticed that she was getting some looks from boys. In fact, they were blatantly staring at her breasts. Then one boy yelled, "Nice ta-tas, Tay-Tay!" The whole class exploded in laughter. Taylor bolted from the gym.

You can just imagine the thoughts, feelings, and actions that Taylor experienced after this event. Horrifying, right? She went from feeling comfortable and fairly confident to thinking, feeling, and acting differently toward herself and her body. With a few words from a stupid guy in gym class, Taylor began viewing her body as an enemy.

In this chapter we'll tap on some of the same things that Taylor tapped on after the gym incident—not just the event itself, but the way she began thinking and feeling about her changing body.

Taylor's experience happened in ninth grade. Whatever grade you're in, as a teenage girl you're probably still growing, changing, and evolving. Tapping is an important tool to keep using as you grow and develop into who you and your body are becoming. As you go through these changes, I ask you to do these tapping exercises to reduce the stress you feel about your body. As you reduce your stress, you will begin to notice that you can have a more positive relationship with your body.

Please take your time in this chapter, because I want to help you resolve the negative thoughts and feelings you have about your body, become more of a friend to your body, and increase your confidence and your appreciation of yourself. Why? Because you're awesome and you deserve to be comfortable and at home in your wonderful body. I want you to be happy in your own skin.

Tapping in the Mirror Exercise

As your body changes, or as you think about ways it's already changed, please notice how you're speaking to yourself about your body. Remember in the last chapter I asked you to notice how you talk to yourself and write down what you're saying to yourself? The time I really want you to notice your self-talk is when you're looking in the mirror.

I know it's weird, but tapping while you're looking in the mirror is an amazing thing to do for yourself each day. In a bit, I'll be giving you some phrases you can say while you're tapping, but first I want you to experiment with simply tapping through the points, or doing the Butterfly Hug, while looking at yourself in the mirror. Doing this will help you become more comfortable with the mirror exercise and then you can add words when you feel ready. The more you do this, the less negative you'll be toward yourself, and you'll become more neutral and even more positive as you look at yourself in the mirror. It's totally possible to get to the point where you like what you see when you look in the mirror!

How Taylor tapped on her thoughts and feelings about her body

I know that some of the setup statements that Taylor and I tapped on, listed below, sound pretty negative, but remember that we create the negative setup statement because we want to tap on what we're actually thinking and feeling. And the setup statements always end with a positive phrase such as "I love and accept myself." It's super important to tap on the negative statements you have taking up space in your mind (and in your stress backpack). Those destructive, unkind thoughts undermine your self-confidence, your well-being, and your happiness—and it's all happening in your mind, so you have the tapping power to change how you're thinking about yourself.

By tapping while looking in the mirror, Taylor totally shifted how she was thinking and feeling about her body and went back to feeling confident and comfortable. You can too!

Karate Chop: Even though I don't like what I see in the mirror right now, I love and accept myself.
Karate Chop: Even though I don't like how I look, I'd rather love and accept myself.
Karate Chop: Even though I'm pretty critical of myself, I'd rather be kinder to myself.

Eyebrow: I don't like what I see in the mirror . . .
Side of Eye: The mirror is not my friend . . .
Under Eye: I'm not liking how I look . . .
Under Nose: And I'm being hard on myself . . .
Chin: I'm being very critical . . .
Collarbone: I'd rather be kinder to myself . . .
Under Arm: I'm focusing on what I don't like . . .
Top of Head: But ignoring what I do like . . .

Keep tapping:

Eyebrow: I'm focusing on this and that . . .
Side of Eye: That I don't like . . .
Under Eye: So that's all I see . . .
Under Nose: That's all I look at . . .
Chin: I'd rather focus attention . . .
Collarbone: On things I like about myself . . .
Under Arm: That I think are okay . . .
Top of Head: What if I focus on what I think is okay about me?

Fill in these blanks yourself:

Eyebrow: My body is pretty amazing . . .
Side of Eye: It can do _____
Under Eye: It can do _____
Under Nose: It can _____
Chin: It can _____
Collarbone: It can _____
Under Arm: It can _____
Top of Head: I appreciate my body for all it can do.

After tapping this round—yes, it's a long one—how are you feeling? Do you feel any different when you look in the mirror? Over time, you might find that your eyes aren't as drawn to parts of you that you've been critical of. And maybe you'll focus more on seeing that you're awesome the way you are!

If you've been harsh on yourself for a long time, try to be patient while you tap to change your habits of thinking when you look in the mirror. Some girls might feel a bit better immediately, some may feel a lot better, and others may need to do this exercise for a week or two before noticing significant changes. Please stick with it.

CASSIDY'S COMMENT

Okay, I know it sounds really weird to tap while looking at yourself in the mirror, but please give it a try! Stick with it and I promise you will feel better! I know so many girls who are so hard on themselves about how they look, and really you can pick any body part from fingernails to body fat and I guarantee that some girl somewhere will hate that part of her. But what's the point of hating a part of yourself? It's stressful, it feels awful, and you have a hard time being happy and confident. Yes, tapping might not change the size of your nose, but I know tapping will help you start seeing that it really doesn't matter!

• •

Think of it as a spa treatment!

In the stress study I talked about earlier, most girls (67 percent) were stressed about some aspect of their appearance. So if I asked you what you don't like about your appearance, what comes to mind? Write down one thing. I don't want you being critical of yourself and making a big list of the things you think are wrong with your appearance.

Think of it as a spa treatment for your body. You're going to tap to create a new, friendly, and loving connection with your body as a whole by tapping away the criticism and tapping in the love for individual parts of your body you've been harsh with.

Taylor specifically tapped on not liking her breasts. You can follow along with her tapping but replace the word *breasts* with whatever body part you're not being friendly toward. I'm not promising that you'll immediately start loving that body part, but if you keep at it you will become more neutral and eventually you'll stop being mean to yourself about it.

Karate Chop: Even though when I look in the mirror, I don't like my breasts, I'd rather be kinder to that part of me.
Karate Chop: Even though when I look in the mirror, I don't like my breasts, I'd rather be kinder to that part of me.
Karate Chop: Even though when I look in the mirror, I don't like my breasts, I'd rather be kinder to that part of me.

Now you're going to repeat the following reminder phrases while tapping on the points. Just replace "breasts" with your own body part. Please make sure you tap all the way to the end.

Eyebrow: I don't like my _____ . . .
Side of Eye: I don't like my breasts . . .
Under Eye: I don't like my breasts . . .
Under Nose: I don't like my breasts . . .
Chin: I don't like my breasts . . .
Collarbone: I don't like my breasts . . .
Under Arm: I don't like my breasts . . .
Top of Head: I'd rather be kinder to my breasts . . .

Keep tapping:

Eyebrow: I'd rather be kinder to my breasts . . .
Side of Eye: I'd rather be kinder to my breasts . . .
Under Eye: I'd rather be kinder to my breasts . . .
Under Nose: I'd rather be kinder to my breasts . . .
Chin: I'd rather be kinder to my breasts . . .
Collarbone: I'd rather be kinder to my breasts . . .
Under Arm: I'd rather be kinder to my breasts . . .
Top of Head: I'd rather be kinder to my breasts and to myself.

Tap until you begin to feel better, then try a super-positive tapping sequence like this:

Eyebrow: I like my breasts . . .
Side of Eye: I appreciate my breasts . . .
Under Eye: I love my breasts . . .
Under Nose: I love my breasts . . .
Chin: I love my breasts . . .
Collarbone: I love my breasts . . .
Under Arm: I love my breasts . . .
Top of Head: I love my breasts . . .

When you're feeling better about this part of your body, pick another body part that you complain about and do the exact same tapping. Bookmark this page and come back to it! If you want to have more confidence in how you look, I believe you need to start with being kinder to yourself about the parts of you that you don't think are 100 percent awesome. So please keep tapping on this subject until you're feeling better about yourself.

If you aren't feeling better yet, give it another try from the beginning. Tap on it again tomorrow, and the next day, until you're feeling less stress about this part of you. Remember, if you've been complaining about it for a long time, it might take a while to tap it out.

. . . .

CASSIDY'S COMMENT

I wasn't sure if it was normal for me to feel uncomfortable about these changes in my body. It was cool to read this and know that other girls feel this way too. But it was even better to tap on this and actually feel more peaceful about what my body's doing. I know it's normal and now I feel more normal.

. . . .

Sometimes people notice your changing body

Along with the changes in your body, sometimes—like Taylor—you also have to deal with other people noticing the changes in your body and thinking it's okay for them to comment on those changes. It can feel embarrassing and uncomfortable and whether it's boys, as in Taylor's case, or girls at school, your parent, or a creepy neighbor who makes a comment—even if it's a compliment—it can leave an unpleasant imprint on you.

Unfortunately in our society, people think they have the right to comment on how other people look. Some of the time what they say is unkind, and an unkind comment can stick to us as if it were the truth. It is not the truth and it certainly is not your truth. Please don't let somebody's stupid, thoughtless comment make you turn on your body. I want you to be friends with your body and be on your body's side.

The way to do that is to tap on the comments that bother you, which is what Taylor did. But before you start tapping, check to see how much the comment is bothering you right now, on a scale of 0 to 10. When you think about the comment someone made, what number would you give it? If you're really creeped out and upset, it might register as a 10 out of 10. If you're mildly creeped out, it might be a 3 or 4 out of 10. Once you've tapped, check in again and see how much the comment bothers you at *that* moment. If you're still feeling bothered, keep tapping until you're feeling more comfortable. Checking in with your level of intensity when you're tapping on something helps you keep track of how good it feels to take charge of these things that are upsetting you.

Karate Chop: Even though they commented on the changes in my body, I love and accept myself.
Karate Chop: Even though they think it was a compliment, it was creepy, and I refuse to give it any meaning.
Karate Chop: Even though that was embarrassing, I love and accept myself.
Karate Chop: Even though I want to hide until I'm an adult, I'd rather be comfortable in my body.

Eyebrow: I can't believe they made that comment . . .
Side of Eye: And they think it's a compliment . . .
Under Eye: I'm so embarrassed . . .
Under Nose: I'm creeped out . . .
Chin: I just want to hide . . .
Collarbone: And it's inappropriate for others to comment . . .
Under Arm: My body is my business . . ."
Top of Head: And not their business.

Tapping Tip: Freestylin' Your Reminder Phrases

When you first learn tapping, it's good to practice reminder phrases that repeat the words from your setup statement while tapping through all the points. That's the basic and effective way to use the reminder phrases, and you can tap that way every time and get great results. But if you want to switch things up, as Cassidy suggested in Chapter 2, I'm giving you full permission to play with the reminder phrases. Think of it as freestylin'.

After you say your setup statement, you can say a basic reminder phrase as you tap a couple of the points and then go into freestylin' mode while still staying on the issue you're focusing on from your setup statement. Lots of girls enjoy freestyle tapping because they really get to express their personality and their sense of humor, as well as their deeper thoughts and feelings, as they tap on a bothersome issue.

You'll notice as you read through the book and do the tapping exercises that I do a lot of freestylin' for you. You'll get a sense of the wide variety of things you can say as you tap, and having this freestyle freedom might get you tapping even more.

You might not be able to keep people from commenting, but you can tap to get relief from the discomfort their words leave you with. And if people make unkind remarks about your body, it's super important that you tap on it and release it.

Taylor had to stop playing that tape over and over in her mind of what the boy in gym class said, and the laughter that followed. If someone has said something to you that was unkind, untrue, inappropriate, creepy, or gross, their opinion is not something you should keep chewing on. Use tapping to spit it out! Use the statements below and fill in the blanks:

Karate Chop: Even though when they said _____, I felt _____, I love and accept myself.

Karate Chop: Even though I can't believe they said that , I love and accept myself.

Karate Chop: Even though when they made that comment about my body, I was pretty grossed out, I love and accept myself anyway.

Karate Chop: Even though when they said _____, I was really embarrassed and they were inappropriate, I love and accept myself.

Karate Chop: Even though they were wrong to say that to me, I'm letting it go and not listening to it again and I love and accept myself.

Karate Chop: Even though they said that, I love and accept myself too much to keep playing that gross tape in my head.

Eyebrow: I can't believe they said that about my _____. . .
Side of Eye: I was really embarrassed when they said that . . .
Under Eye: It wasn't okay that they said that . . .
Under Nose: That was inappropriate . . .
Chin: I can't believe they said _____. . .
Collarbone: Don't they know how inappropriate that was . . . ?

Under Arm: I'm choosing not to listen to that in my head . . .
Top of Head: There's no room for what they said . . .

Eyebrow: I'm not playing that tape in my head anymore . . .
Side of Eye: I will not believe what they said . . .
Under Eye: It was hurtful and stupid . . .
Under Nose: And I reject what they said . . .
Chin: Instead of rejecting myself . . .
Collarbone: I am going to be kind to myself . . .
Under Arm: And not repeat that comment to myself . . .
Top of Head: I love and respect myself too much.

"I get stressed when I compare myself to others"

Do you compare yourself to other girls? What about comparing yourself to air-brushed photos of girls and women who've been professionally styled and made up? Stressful, right? In the survey about stress, most teenage girls reported that they feel bad when they compare themselves to other people, especially on social media. I know you won't stay away from social media, but what if you can use tapping to help you neutralize the unhelpful thinking you might be doing when comparing yourself to the other people you encounter there?

Let's try this exercise of filling in the blanks with your feelings and creating setup statements. Grab your notebook and write down some ideas. You can use the examples I've given you or make up your own.

When I look at pictures of models, I feel _____.
When I look at girls at school, I feel _____.
When I compare myself to other girls, I feel _____.
When I see people's pictures on social media, I feel _____.

Karate Chop: Even though when I look at models I feel _____, I love and accept myself.
Karate Chop: Even though when I look at girls at school I feel bad about myself, I'd rather love and accept myself now.
Karate Chop: Even though when I compare myself to other girls, I feel like I'll never be good enough, I'd rather love and accept myself now.

Karate Chop: Even though those images are everywhere, I'd rather love and accept myself now.
Karate Chop: Even though it doesn't feel good to compare, I'd rather love and accept myself now.

Eyebrow: I keep comparing myself to how other girls look . . .
Side of Eye: And I never feel good when I do that . . .
Under Eye: I compare myself to pictures of airbrushed models . . .
Under Nose: And I'm really harsh with myself . . .
Chin: About my own looks . . .
Collarbone: I feel like I'll never look as good . . .
Under Arm: As an airbrushed model . . .
Top of Head: I'd rather be kinder to myself . . .

Eyebrow: It doesn't feel good to compare myself . . .
Side of Eye: With other girls . . .
Under Eye: I keep telling myself . . .
Under Nose: That I don't measure up . . .
Chin: Why would I keep telling myself that?
Collarbone: I love and respect myself too much . . .
Under Arm: To keep being unkind to myself . . .
Top of Head: I'm going to be kinder to myself . . .

. . . .

CASSIDY'S COMMENT

I know it is really easy to look at a picture of an actress or musician or other public figure and compare yourself to her. It is also easy to feel bad about yourself after doing this. Tapping is a great way to feel better about yourself and be kinder to yourself.

. . . .

Okay, we're moving on to other health topics. We're still on the topic of the stuff that's going on in your body, and now we're going to talk and tap about the time of the month, your period! Hooray! I'm sure you just love talking about it, but we're going to tap about it now. So if you get crampy and emotional when you have your period, keep on reading . . . and tapping.

There's More to Explore

There's more tapping for you about how you feel about your body. Page 180 has some more setup statements for you to help you feel better in the body you're running around in right now.

TAPFIRMATION

I love and accept myself the way I am!

Chapter 5

TAPPING ABOUT THAT TIME OF THE MONTH

When I was a teenage girl and started my period, I remember complaining to my mother about how uncomfortable and sometimes painful it was. Her response was, "Well, it wasn't meant for your entertainment, dear." That was not helpful. I wanted comfort and maybe some sympathy, and some insight into how I could feel better. I wish I had known about tapping then!

The fact is, this is a thing that has always occurred in the bodies of women and girls and it's the most natural female function. I'm not going to talk about the biology of menstruation, but I am going to offer you some tapping solutions for some of the physical and emotional discomforts associated with your period. Even though there is a hormonal reason that you might have mood fluctuations, physical cramps, or other discomfort, please try tapping for these symptoms.

· ·

CASSIDY'S COMMENT

Yup, we're going there! So many things that come with your period really suck, like cramps and headaches and feeling like someone has messed with your emotions. Tapping is a great way to deal with these. It has really helped me. Tapping is also a great way to help you feel more comfortable with the other changes your body will go through when you first get your period. So if you are feeling uncomfortable, tap!

· ·

Cramps are the worst!

I'm going to give you a bunch of setup statements that relate to cramps. (Fun, right?) Please tap on the ones that apply to you and your symptoms. You might do one phrase three times, especially if this is one of your main complaints. Remember that each person is unique and make sure you change the wording to reflect *your* experience with cramps. You might even find that your experience, and your setup statements, will change month by month.

Do this exercise even if you're not having your period right now! Tapping now might calm future discomfort—seriously. If you usually get cramps, tapping now might help to calm and change that. Of course, if you *are* having symptoms now, tap away! You'll notice that I've done some freestylin' for you with the reminder phrases.

Karate Chop: Even though I have these awful cramps, I love and accept myself.
Karate Chop: Even though I feel like I want to barf with this discomfort, I love and accept myself.
Karate Chop: Even though my lower back is aching, I love and accept myself.
Karate Chop: Even though I feel bloated, I love and accept myself.
Karate Chop: Even though I feel so achy, I'd rather feel relaxed.
Karate Chop: Even though the pain is a bit of a shocker, I love and accept myself.
Karate Chop: Even though I'm uncomfortable, it's normal and I'd rather feel comfortable.
Karate Chop: Even though my breasts hurt and ache, I'd rather feel comfortable.
Karate Chop: Even though even my legs hurt, I love and accept myself.
Karate Chop: Even though these cramps feel like my insides are being gnawed at, I love and accept myself.

Eyebrow: These cramps are awful . . .
Side of Eye: I feel so gross right now . . .
Under Eye: It's like clenching or squeezing . . .
Under Nose: Even my legs hurt . . .
Chin: I want to barf . . .
Collarbone: I'd rather relax in my body
Under Arm: And release the pain . . .
Top of Head: My insides are being gnawed at . . .

Eyebrow: It feels so intense . . .
Side of Eye: It's such a surprise . . .
Under Eye: Even my boobs hurt . . .
Under Nose: It's all normal . . .
Chin: I'd rather be relaxed in my body . . .
Collarbone: My body knows what it's doing . . .
Under Arm: I'd rather be comfortable while it's happening . . .
Top of Head: I give myself permission to be comfortable . . .

Sophia thought something was wrong with her

The first time it happened, Sophia thought something was seriously wrong with her. Her legs were wobbly and her insides were being gnawed at by some beast and she really thought she would barf. Each month after that, Sophia stayed home from school and stayed in bed, curled around a heating pad. Fortunately her mom knew she was having symptoms associated with the start of her period. After a couple months of this, her mom suggested that she try some tapping on her pain and discomfort. Sophia had always made fun of her mom's tapping, but she was desperate and willing to try anything.

I'm going to show you what they tapped on and what you can tap on. I'll put it all in the chart below to show you the different aspects—the thoughts, feelings, and actions—associated with that time of the month. Remember that you can pull a tapping target from your chart, create a setup statement and a reminder phrase, and jump right into tapping.

Event	Thought	Feeling	Action
Something happens	You have a thought	That creates a feeling	You do something
Wobbly pain	There's something wrong with me!	Fear	I curl up with a heating pad
Started period	This isn't fair	Frustration	I stay home from school

Each box represents a tapping topic and Sophia tapped on all these events, thoughts, feelings, and actions. I know you've got this, but I'll give you the eight setup statements for these topics anyway. You can freestyle your way through the reminder phrases while you tap the points.

Karate Chop: Even though I have this wobbly pain, I love and accept myself.

Karate Chop: Even though there's something wrong with me, I love and accept myself.

Karate Chop: Even though I have this fear that something's wrong with me, I love and accept myself.

Karate Chop: Even though I want to curl up with a heating pad, I love and accept myself.

Karate Chop: Even though I've started my period, I love and accept myself.

Karate Chop: Even though this isn't fair, I am still awesome.

Karate Chop: Even though I'm so frustrated, I love and accept myself.

Karate Chop: Even though I want to stay home from school, I still love and accept myself.

Within an hour or so, Sophia's symptoms had subsided and she was feeling much better. When she had a twinge of a cramp Sophia would tap on that event and that too would subside. She went back to school that afternoon, feeling fine. But the really great news here is that the next month, Sophia had no symptoms whatsoever when her period started.

Sophia told me, "I was always teasing my mom about her tapping on everything and she'd pretty much stopped telling me to tap on stuff. But I was desperate after a few months of these awful cramps and that's what made me try it. Now I tap on everything all the time, and now I'm the one reminding my mom to tap herself. So for all you teenage girls reading this, don't wait, start tapping now. Forget about how it looks, or that your mom's been bugging you to try it. I know it doesn't look cool, but it works, and I've never had bad cramps again."

"I get so emotional!"

I know that sometimes you might feel physically awful during your time of the month. Lots of girls have bad menstrual cramps and feel sick. You might get super emotional and it can seem like there's no real reason for your upset. But even if it doesn't make sense, the fact is you're feeling highly emotional, so we're going to do some tapping about that. Check in with the level of intensity of your emotions and give them a number on a scale of 0 to 10. Wanting to scream at someone is likely a 10 out of 10. After tapping, check in with your emotions again and see if they've shifted at all.

Let's make a chart about the emotional stuff that might be happening.

Event	Thought	Feeling	Action
Something happens	You have a thought	That creates a feeling	You do something
Someone says, "You must be on your period"	People are really bugging me	I feel so sensitive	I want to scream at someone

Karate Chop: Even though it bugs me when they say, "You must have your period, you're so cranky," I'm going to ignore them.

Karate Chop: Even though people are really bothering me right now, I love and accept myself.

Karate Chop: Even though I feel extra-sensitive right now, I'd rather feel calm and comfortable.

Karate Chop: Even though I know it's hormonal, I still want to scream at someone, but I love and accept myself.

Eyebrow: They said, "You must have your period" . . .
Side of Eye: But I still want to scream . . .
Under Eye: I feel so sensitive right now . . .
Under Nose: Yes, I am feeling cranky . . .
Chin: Everything is bugging me right now . . .
Collarbone: This emotional roller coaster . . .
Under Arm: I'm so up and down today . . .
Top of Head: I'd rather feel calmer . . .

Eyebrow: I feel so irritated . . .
Side of Eye: I don't have a lot of patience . . .
Under Eye: I just want to stay in bed today . . .

Under Nose: I feel like I'm going to burst into tears . . .
Chin: That's okay . . .
Collarbone: I'd rather be kinder to myself . . .
Under Arm: And take care of myself . . .
Top of Head: I'd rather feel calm and comfortable.

"Skin problems are getting under my skin"

. . . .

CASSIDY'S COMMENT

Sometimes it can feel like the world will end because of one pimple, but some girls have full-on acne and feel like it's ruining their lives. It's like wearing a mask that you can't take off and then trying to put a mask on over that mask to try to cover it. Lots of girls get bullied because of their skin and feel really bad about themselves, trying to hide away. So if you're feeling bad because of something that's going on with your skin, do this tapping and hopefully you'll feel a bit less stressed about it. After tapping, it might seem like it's okay to relax from focusing so harshly on your skin. Believe me, this will be a relief. And remember, you're not alone; lots of girls know what you're going through.

. . . .

I think it's normal to have breakouts on your skin, and some teenage girls have more than others; some might break out especially around their menstrual cycles. There's lots of information out there about the cleansers, lotions, and treatments you can use if you have acne or other skin problems. You can also use tapping—not only to help heal the pimples, but to get some relief from the emotional pressure of having breakouts on your skin. When you look at yourself in the mirror, that might be the first thing you see, and you might think your skin is all anybody is looking at. That adds even more stress, so you can tap on that.

Karate Chop: Even though I have these spots on my face, I love and accept myself.
Karate Chop: Even though I'm so frustrated with my skin, I love and accept myself.
Karate Chop: Even though I've tried everything on my skin and I'm so frustrated, I love and accept myself.

Eyebrow: I have these spots on my face . . .
Side of Eye: I'm so frustrated with my skin . . .
Under Eye: I've tried everything on my skin . . .
Under Nose: I'm so frustrated . . .
Chin: I feel frustrated with these spots . . .
Collarbone: I don't know what else to do . . .
Under Arm: I'd rather feel calmer about my skin . . .
Top of Head: I'd rather have calmer skin.

A pimple is an event

Event	Thought	Feeling	Action
Something happens	You have a thought	That creates a feeling	You do something
I wake up to a pimple	That's all anybody will see	I feel so ugly	I cry

Karate Chop: Even though I have this pimple and I know that's all anybody is looking at, I love and accept myself.
Karate Chop: Even though I feel so ugly, I want to love and accept myself.
Karate Chop: Even though I burst into tears when I saw that pimple, I still love and accept myself.

Eyebrow: I just want to cry . . .
Side of Eye: It is the end of the world . . .
Under Eye: This stupid pimple . . .
Under Nose: Life-ruining pimple . . .
Chin: I feel so ugly . . .
Collarbone: People will stare at this monolith . . .
Under Arm: That's all they'll see . . .
Top of Head: I'd rather feel calmer.

See how you can really tap for anything? When you do your reminder phrases, using the language that you'd typically use will really help you decrease the drama about that breakout.

• •

CASSIDY'S COMMENT

How did you do? Tapping is pretty easy, right? Did you ever think you could actually get relief and comfort about that time of the month? And it will keep being that easy because you tap the same way every time. As you read the rest of the book, some of the things you might tap on may get more serious or dramatic. But tapping will always be there for you, to help you feel better. Keep going!

• •

There's More to Explore

If you want to do some more tapping on how you feel about that time of the month, there are more tapping solution phrases for you on page 182.

TAPFIRMATION

I'd rather feel comfortable while my body's doing its thing.

Chapter 6

TAPPING ABOUT YOUR EMOTIONAL HEALTH

This whole book is about tapping for your emotional health. In fact, tapping is also called Emotional Freedom Techniques (EFT), so improving your emotional health is built into tapping. Increasing your sense of calm, peace, joy, fun, and excitement is what this book is about. But I also wanted you to have a chapter where we talk and tap specifically about stuff that can interfere with our emotional health, like worries, anxiety, fears, and grief.

· ·

CASSIDY'S COMMENT

Okay, girls, you've *got* to stop worrying about everything, 'cause worrying sucks! Don't know how to stop worrying? This is your chapter for tapping! Worrying is so stressful and you can't fully enjoy the great parts of your life if you're worrying about the things you can't control right now. You can't celebrate being your awesome self when you're worrying about life. So, take your time through this chapter and abolish worry from your to-do list!

· ·

"I worry about everything!"

On some days, that probably sums up the way you feel pretty well. So let's dive right in!

Karate Chop: Even though I worry about everything, I love and accept myself.
Karate Chop: Even though I worry about everything, I love and accept myself.
Karate Chop: Even though I worry about everything, I love and accept myself.

Eyebrow: I worry about everything!
Side of Eye: I worry about everything!
Under Eye: I worry about everything!
Under Nose: I worry about everything!
Chin: I worry about everything!
Collarbone: I worry about everything!
Under Arm: I worry about everything!
Top of Head: I worry about everything!

A big ball of elastic bands

The reason I want to get you tapping on this all-encompassing topic is because many girls can't even pinpoint what it is they're worried about. This makes me think of a giant worry ball of elastic bands. Picture it: a ball of elastic bands with several different colors entangled with one another. The way I think of it is that all the blue elastic bands represent a specific worry, all the yellow ones represent a different worry, and the red ones, a separate worry again.

When the elastics are wound up together, they can feel very overwhelming. Imagine holding this worry ball in your hand. It would be pretty heavy and dense, right?

By tapping on "I worry about everything," I think we can begin to pull apart the elastic bands and then use tapping on some of the specific worries that might be bothering you.

CASSIDY'S COMMENT

I love this idea of the big ball of worry, with each color representing a different worry. It's like that knot you get in your stomach when you're going through exams. Each exam is a colored elastic band and the whole week of exams is a big ball of elastic bands all tangled up together. When I tap on exams, I picture the big ball unraveling, and the small individual elastic bands lined up in a row. You may be worried about math but feel pretty confident about English. It's hard to feel confident about something when it's all tangled up in this big ball of stuff. Everything seems so much worse when it is one big pile of unorganized mess.

Visualization Tapping Exercise

Take a few minutes and see if you can picture your own ball of elastic bands of worry. Notice the colors and try to assign a specific worry to each color you see. Lots of people say this helps them to separate the different worries they have, which feels less overwhelming than worrying about everything. Then you can tap about each of the specific worries that you've identified:

Even though I have this yellow worry about my English exam . . .
Even though I have this red worry about the world . . .

I think it's a great way to think more creatively about worry and this can help with the feelings of overwhelm when you look at all your worries wrapped up together in a giant ball.

You can tap on any of the specific worries that are bothering you right now and anything you've worried about in the past. The tapping targets below and in the back of the book represent things that teenage girls tend to worry about. Feel free to tap on anything that feels like it might spark a tinge of worry in you.

"I worry about what's going on in the world"

Sometimes it happens in the classroom while studying current events. Or you see a news story about something that's happened on the other side of the world. Or you're aware that your community has a large homeless population. Some of your thoughts about this might be:

- The world is a scary place.
- I'm not safe.
- What if that bad thing happened here/to me?
- How could those things happen to people?
- I feel so bad for those people.
- I can't stop seeing the images from that news report.

It's easy to turn these thoughts into tapping setup statements. Pick something you're thinking (worrying) about:

- When I think about _____ I feel _____
- When I think about what I saw on the news, I feel so bad for those people.
- When I think about those tragedies, I feel helpless.

And make it part of your setup statement:

Karate Chop: Even though when I think about what I saw on the news, I feel so bad for those people, I love and accept myself.

Karate Chop: Even though I keep thinking about these tragedies, I love and accept myself.

Karate Chop: Even though I feel helpless when I think about these tragedies, I love and accept myself.

Karate Chop: Even though I can't get those pictures out of my head, I'd rather picture good things for those people.

Karate Chop: Even though it's painful to think about those people, I'd rather send them love.

Eyebrow: There are some scary things happening in the world . . .
Side of Eye: I've been thinking about these bad things that happen . . .
Under Eye: It isn't helping me to think about these things . . .
Under Nose: And it isn't helping these people I'm worrying about . . .
Chin: Thinking about those tragedies is painful . . .
Collarbone: But it's nothing compared to what they're going through . . .
Under Arm: I can't get those pictures out of my head . . .
Top of Head: Instead of worrying about them, I'd rather wish good things for them.

Are you carrying the weight of the world?

Have you ever heard the phrase "She's carrying the weight of the world on her shoulders"? Think about what that means for a minute. I want to help you understand the difference between carrying the weight of the world on your shoulders and having sympathy, empathy, and compassion for others. We've talked about your stress backpack and how heavy that can be when you're not finding ways to alleviate the stress you're experiencing in your day-to-day life.

When you feel sympathy for someone, you're consciously aware that someone else is having a tough time. Having empathy for another's situation means that you are putting yourself in their shoes, and you may even experience their pain or upset as if the same thing is happening to you. Feeling compassion for someone goes deeper than empathy in that you want to take some kind of action to help alleviate another's suffering. Having sympathy, empathy, and compassion for others can help you feel more connected to the other humans and other creatures on the planet.

The weight of the world is a different kind of stress because it is not your stress, but you're carrying it in addition to what's already in your stress backpack. Carrying the weight of the world on your shoulders is a direct result of thinking, and worrying, about things that are happening to other people that you don't feel you can help with. You can feel powerless when you're burdening yourself with worries this way. I think that weight-of-the-world stress occurs when sympathy, empathy, and compassion for others overrides taking care of your own stress and your own needs. You can have compassion for others and for yourself at the same time.

Lots of young women tell me they can't stop thinking about something that has happened to someone else, sometimes to a friend and sometimes to someone on the other side of the world. Some girls have a fear of something similar happening to them or to their friends or family. They admit that they spend a lot of time thinking about horrible events or atrocities.

When I ask them how it feels when they spend time thinking about these things, not one person tells me they feel great. Each person feels bad when thinking about negative world events. It makes sense, though, right? When you are spending a lot of time thinking about negative things, how can you possibly feel good?

Many people argue that if they stop thinking about these negative world events, and the people who are hurt by them, then they are being selfish. They even say that the least they can do is think and worry about these events and people. They feel guilty if they're not worrying about others and some even think they deserve to carry this weight of the world.

But you know, logically, that worrying about others doesn't actually help them in any way, and there are actions you can take that *will* be helpful to people who are going through difficulties. Worry and guilt are feelings and thoughts that you're experiencing and they are stressors taking up space in your stress backpack. Instead of helping anyone else with your guilt and worry, you're actually stressing and harming yourself. Tapping will help you calm the disruptive feelings and make more positive decisions about helping others.

Karate Chop: Even though I understand that someone else is hurting, and I can have sympathy, I love and accept myself.
Karate Chop: Even though I can even imagine how someone else's pain might feel, and I can have empathy, I love and accept myself.
Karate Chop: Even though I keep putting myself in their situation and it's becoming difficult to be happy, I love and accept myself.
Karate Chop: Even though I know that someone else is hurting, I'd rather have compassion and send them love and good wishes.

Eyebrow: I have sympathy that they are going through something painful . . .
Side of Eye: I can imagine how they feel and it's an awful feeling . . .
Under Eye: I keep putting myself in their situation and it feels awful . . .
Under Nose: They must really be suffering . . .
Chin: Sometimes I think I should suffer because so many people are suffering . . .
Collarbone: But when I'm suffering it's hard to concentrate on my work and on my life . . .

Under Arm: I wonder if there is some other way I can help without suffering . . .
Top of Head: I can have compassion and send love . . .

Eyebrow: That event must have been horrible to experience . . .
Side of Eye: I can imagine how that must have been for them . . .
Under Eye: I can see those pictures in my mind right now . . .
Under Nose: But when I see those pictures, I feel stressed . . .
Chin: I'd like to erase those images from my mind . . .
Collarbone: Feeling bad isn't helping me . . .
Under Arm: And I'm not helping anyone by feeling bad . . .
Top of Head: I'd rather have compassion and send them love . . .

I believe we can be more helpful, have more compassion, and care for others better when we are feeling good. When we release the weight of the world from our shoulders, we can see the events in the world without having to feel them deeply—without having to go there in our minds and hearts. We can observe and witness and, from a place of peace, send them love. When we have a sense of peace within ourselves, we may have more insight into what other kinds of actions we might be able to take to help people in bad situations.

Kaylee couldn't stop worrying about the tragedy across the world

Kaylee was in ninth grade when the earthquake and tsunami hit Japan in 2011. There was a shocking video in the news and she kept searching online for more to watch. It seemed like her head was filled with these frightening images. At first she was sympathetic and thought how awful it must be for the people involved. But as she watched more and more of the videos, she began to put herself in similar circumstances in her imagination because her own home was in an area that was referred to as an earthquake zone. She didn't sleep at all that night and she couldn't get the images out of her head, or her dreams.

The next day, her school did emergency preparedness classes. For some of her friends, that was helpful; they liked the idea of having a plan and good information if they ever were hit with an earthquake. But for Kaylee, it increased her stress because now she was imagining horrible events like those in Japan affecting her and her loved ones.

Initially Kaylee had hoped there would be something she could do to help. But her sympathy for the people struggling became overwhelming when she imagined herself in similar circumstances and spent hours watching images of the devastation that followed the earthquake and tsunami. Not only was she worried about the people affected in Japan, she was even more worried about her own family. She was overwhelmed.

Tapping helped Kaylee calm her global worry as well as her personal worry and helped her come up with a plan. As you can imagine, her level of intensity and upset were 10 out of 10 when she started tapping.

Karate Chop: Even though what happened in Japan was horrible, I love and accept myself.
Karate Chop: Even though that happened so far away, I feel for the people affected and I love and accept myself anyway.
Karate Chop: Even though I got those horrible images stuck in my head and I can't stop thinking about it, I love and accept myself.

Eyebrow: What happened was horrible . . .
Side of Eye: I feel for the people affected . . .
Under Eye: I wanted to help them somehow . . .
Under Nose: But I got overwhelmed by the images . . .
Chin: I can't stop thinking about it . . .
Collarbone: I keep worrying about it happening here . . .
Under Arm: I don't know what I'd do if it happened here . . .
Top of Head: I'd love to get those images out of my head . . .

Eyebrow: Those images are stuck in my head . . .
Side of Eye: Of cars and buildings being swept away . . .
Under Eye: It's okay to let go of the images . . .
Under Nose: I don't need to keep seeing things that feel so awful . . .
Chin: To have compassion for the people affected . . .
Collarbone: I'd rather picture them doing well and being happy . . .
Under Arm: I'd rather picture myself being prepared in case something were to happen . . .
Top of Head: I'd rather feel calm.

Kaylee kept tapping this way until she felt calmer. She was then able to talk calmly with her parents about putting together an emergency plan for their home. She was able to have compassion for people without imagining herself painfully in their circumstances. And over the following weeks, she did odd jobs, collected recycling, and raised money to send to a relief fund for people affected by the earthquake in Japan.

CASSIDY'S COMMENT

How do you feel about worrying? If you can break this habit, you'll have a lot more space in your mind to think about the things you want to achieve in your life. Had I not found tapping and stopped worrying about everything, I don't think that I would be the person I am today or have accomplished the things I have. I know some girls think about something they really, really want, but they never try to do what they can to get it because they are worried that they will fail. But when you tap on that worry you're free to think about achieving the thing you want. For example, when I tapped and stopped worrying about whether or not I'd get on the basketball team, then I was able to play better, be relaxed, and have more fun. Guess what? I made the team. I know I was able to do my best because I wasn't worried about doing my best. Make sense? It can work for you too! But you have to do the tapping for it to actually work. Reading about it isn't enough.

Worry can lead to anxiety

Being worried about things causes stress and can contribute to feelings of anxiety. When you feel anxious, what do you notice? Maybe your mind is full of stuff, making it difficult to find solutions because you're running in circles on the hamster wheel of doom. You might also have physical symptoms in your body. Your heart might beat faster, your chest might feel tight, and you might find it hard to take a deep breath. Often people use the word *anxious* to describe feeling afraid, freaked out, and so on. But whatever word you're using, and whatever you're feeling in your body, please tap on those feelings. I'll show you how.

Karate Chop: Even though I feel anxious, I love and accept myself.
Karate Chop: Even though I have this tightness in my chest, I love and accept myself.
Karate Chop: Even though my heart seems like it's racing, I love and accept myself.
Karate Chop: Even though it's hard to take a deep breath, I love and accept myself.

Eyebrow: My chest is tight . . .
Side of Eye: My heart's racing . . .
Under Eye: Hard to take a deep breath . . .
Under Nose: My chest is tight . . .
Chin: My heart's racing . . .
Collarbone: Hard to take a deep breath . . .
Under Arm: I'd rather feel calm . . .
Top of Head: I'd rather feel peaceful.

You can tap anytime it occurs to you that you're feeling anxious. And as you go through this book, you might also notice that other words, feelings, and ideas better express your unique feelings.

What are you so afraid of?

Anybody, at any age, can experience fear about situations, like dating, taking exams, speaking in class, or things like dogs, spiders, and so on. What I know about fear is that fear can keep you from doing things in your life. Fear can, of course, keep you from putting your hand on a hot stove for fear of burning yourself, which is a great role for fear to play in your life. But what I want to help you with is anything you're afraid of doing that is *interfering* with your life.

As you go through the earlier part of this chapter that gives tapping solutions for stuff you're worrying about, you might also realize that some of the things you're worrying about are also things you're afraid of. For example, if you're afraid of dogs, you might worry that you'll run into a dog on your way to school. Having the fear of dogs is a stress that you're carrying around in your backpack, and then worrying about running into a dog is another stressor. Tapping can help you resolve the fear and also the worry. You might want to grab your notebook and write down things you're afraid of.

I'm afraid of _____.

Please don't judge yourself or your fear. Right now we're getting material to tap on because anything on your list instantly becomes a setup statement. So whether you're afraid of ghosts, the future, or talking to someone you have a crush on, put that in your own setup statement. Then measure your level of intensity on a scale of 0 to 10 and write that down.

Karate Chop: Even though I'm afraid of _____t, I love and accept myself.

Makayla hated snakes!

Makayla was terrified of snakes. Even looking at a picture of a snake would freak her out and she'd start crying. Now, at 14 years old, she had an opportunity to be a team leader at a cool summer camp where there would be lots of outdoor activities. But she was going to turn it down, thinking there would be snakes there. She was ready to say no but she did some tapping instead. She started simply: *Even though I'm afraid of snakes, I love and accept myself.* While tapping her karate chop, she repeated this phrase over and over, determined to get some relief.

That's when she remembered her older brother handing her a can that looked like a can of potato chips. She was eight years old at the time and was surprised that her big brother was offering her a snack; he never shared anything with her. She was opening the tin, her mouth watering, when the fake snake jumped out at her. She wasn't just startled, she was floored.

So she tapped on that event, realizing that this was why she was so afraid of snakes now.

Karate Chop: Even though my brother offered me that treat and it was a snake, I love and accept myself.
Karate Chop: Even though I never got over that, I love and accept myself.
Karate Chop: Even though that happened, I'm okay now.
Karate Chop: Even though he scared the crap out of me, and it wasn't even a real snake, I love and accept myself.
Karate Chop: Even though it wasn't even a real snake, somehow I'm afraid of snakes and I love and accept myself.
Karate Chop: Even though he was pretending to be nice but he was really mean, I love and accept myself.

Makayla spent some time tapping on all these phrases and realized that she was really upset with her brother. She still didn't trust him, so she did some tapping on that as well. She was super brave then and actually searched for images of snakes online, tapping all the while. When she felt ready, she opened her eyes and clicked on an image. To her surprise, she didn't burst into tears. She kept tapping and felt more and more comfortable. Then she searched for an image of snakes in a can and tapped on that as well.

When you think of things that you're afraid of, do you know when that fear began? You can even ask your parents or people who've known you a long time if they remember. Keep tapping on your fears and you'll begin to notice that you feel braver when you think about doing new things.

Grieving for someone or something you've lost

It's normal to feel sadness because a loved one has died or a relationship has ended. Feeling sadness is a part of the grieving process and it's important to acknowledge your feelings as your own. Your grief and sadness is unique, just as your relationship with your loved one who died was unique.

Sometimes people think that they're supposed to feel sad for a long time after someone has died and so they hesitate to do some tapping on their sadness. But if you find that your sadness is interfering with living your own life and enjoying your life, then I do recommend some tapping.

Tapping on this kind of sadness does not interfere with your happy memories of your loved one, and you will probably agree that they would have wanted you to feel happy again, and enjoy your life. I'd like you to give yourself permission to do some tapping on your sadness and move toward feeling happy again.

Karate Chop: Even though when I think about my granddad dying, I feel sad, I love and accept myself anyway.
Karate Chop: Even though I will miss him and I am sad about that, I love and accept myself.
Karate Chop: Even though it's my first experience with someone dying, I love and accept myself.

Eyebrow: He passed away . . .
Side of Eye: And I feel sad . . .

Under Eye: It's normal to feel sad . . .
Under Nose: He was really kind and funny . . .
Chin: I really loved him . . .
Collarbone: I really miss him . . .
Under Arm: I have some good memories of him . . .
Top of Head: But my sadness has taken over . . .

Eyebrow: He would want me to be happy . . .
Side of Eye: I thought I could never be happy again . . .
Under Eye: But sometimes I'll laugh at something . . .
Under Nose: And feel guilty about it . . .
Chin: It's okay to laugh and be happy again . . .
Collarbone: He would want that . . .
Under Arm: He would want me to be happy . . .
Top of Head: I give myself permission to be happy.

Being a sensitive person

I mentioned earlier that one of the main things I heard growing up was that I was being too sensitive. In looking back I see I was super sensitive. My feelings got hurt easily and I often was told I shouldn't have hurt feelings about whatever had hurt me. It wasn't just that I was an emotional teenage girl, I was a *sensitive* teenage girl and the people around me didn't understand that. My parents were annoyed by my sensitivity and my sisters teased me about it. So I grew up believing it was bad to be so sensitive.

I know now that if tapping had been invented when I was a sensitive teenage girl, life would have been much easier. I would have been able to tap on the hurt feelings I had when I was being teased and taunted. I wish I had tapping to help me back then because I felt things very deeply. So please, if you are a sensitive girl like me, tap for yourself.

Then when someone says you're too sensitive, you can say to them, "I am sensitive, but because of that, I'm also super creative. I'm empathetic toward people because I am sensitive to their emotions, which makes me a great friend and a great listener. And sometimes I am so sensitive that I get startled—loud noises and harsh smells bother me and I might get overwhelmed more easily than you. But I'm awesome."

Karate Chop: Even though they tell me to stop being so sensitive, I don't know how, but I love and accept myself.

Karate Chop: Even though they tease me about being sensitive, I love and accept myself.

Karate Chop: Even though being sensitive might mean that I get hurt feelings, I love and accept myself.

Karate Chop: Even though insensitive people tell me not to be so sensitive, I love and accept myself.

Karate Chop: Even though being sensitive means that I feel things more deeply, I love and accept myself.

Karate Chop: Even though being sensitive means that I might get startled easily, I love and accept myself.

Eyebrow:	They tell me not to be so sensitive . . .
Side of Eye:	I feel things deeply . . .
Under Eye:	I still want to feel deeply . . .
Under Nose:	But sometimes it's painful . . .
Chin:	It's not a flaw to be sensitive . . .
Collarbone:	I might get startled . . .
Under Arm:	I might have a strong reaction to something . . .
Top of Head:	I'd rather feel more peaceful . . .

Imagine you're talking to someone about your sensitivity.

Eyebrow:	Just because it didn't hurt your feelings . . .
Side of Eye:	Doesn't mean it didn't hurt my feelings . . .
Under Eye:	I'm more sensitive to insults . . .
Under Nose:	And when you're upset or hurting . . .
Chin:	I'm sensitive enough to notice . . .
Collarbone:	Sometimes being sensitive is painful for me . . .
Under Arm:	I'm hoping to quiet my sensitivity . . .
Top of Head:	So that I'm more comfortable and peaceful . . .

Eyebrow:	But I'm glad I'm sensitive . . .
Side of Eye:	I'm empathetic toward people . . .
Under Eye:	I might get overwhelmed . . .
Under Nose:	But I feel things deeply . . .

Chin: Yes, my feelings get hurt . . .
Collarbone: But I have deep feelings . . .
Under Arm: I love being sensitive . . .
Top of Head: I love me and my sensitivity.

I know this will help you feel better. It might be something you have to go back to and tap on regularly. Please take time to tap about being sensitive and soon you'll come to appreciate this quality in yourself. I know, because that's what I did.

There's More to Explore
If you'd like to do some tapping about more emotional health topics, you can visit page 185 and explore more.

TAPFIRMATION
I can have compassion for others while being happy in my life.

part three

TAPPING ON STUFF THAT HAPPENS AT HOME

· ·

CASSIDY'S COMMENT

This could be a big, life-changing section for you if your family is going through fighting, separating, divorcing, or any sort of upheaval. You have to tap on every single thing in this part of the book. Parents' fighting is awful—it can really affect you but you don't have a lot of control over it. Next time you can hear your parents fighting, tap. Remind yourself that you are okay.

· ·

Chapter 7

TAPPING ABOUT YOUR PARENTS' RELATIONSHIP

When Kayla was 14 and her parents were arguing all the time, she told her friend that she wouldn't be surprised if they got a divorce. Part of her was hoping they would, because she couldn't stand their arguing. It stressed her out so much. She tried to drown out their voices with loud music on her headphones, but she was also super sensitive to the bad energy in the house. The stress was affecting her schoolwork, and she desperately wanted to tell her parents to stop fighting, but she didn't want to get in the middle of things and risk making them angry at her as well as at each other.

But even though she half expected them to split up, it was still a shock when they made the announcement.

I'm so glad Kayla and I got to tap together during this time because it really helped her deal with the upsetting thoughts and feelings that kept surfacing as things unfolded with her parents. I'll share with you what we worked on together because I think it will help you if your family is going through a similar thing.

Kayla and I worked together as her parents were divorcing, and then, unexpectedly and quickly, her father was in a new relationship. Well, you can imagine that was a challenge for Kayla. She was worried about her mother, she didn't like her dad's new girlfriend, and she really didn't like the girlfriend's kids. So in a very short time, Kayla went from living at home with both her parents to going back and forth between her parents, living with a new stepfamily in their house part-time, and feeling like she had to be okay with everything that was happening.

Does any of Kayla's story sound familiar? Are you feeling stressed out because your family is going through something similar? If so, this chapter is definitely for you.

No matter how it comes about, divorce is a terribly stressful time for everyone involved. Yes, it's a difficult time for your parents, but your job right now is to take care of yourself. I want to give you as much tapping help as I can. If this is something that's happening now, the best thing you can do is tap on the points as often as you can. Put a sticky note somewhere that just says TAP, or put a reminder on your phone that pops up and says TAP. Don't worry about the words—just tap!

Even if the divorce in your family happened a long time ago, it's a good idea to go through these tapping exercises to help you resolve old hurts that you may not realize are still bubbling in the background.

How does their arguing affect you?

When you hear the first signs of an argument between your parents, chances are you're not taking note of what you're thinking and feeling. Your whole system just jumps into a physical reaction. That's how Kayla reacted. So we started by tapping on her *actions* in response to an argument:

Event	Action
Something happens	You do something
Parents are fighting	I slam the door of my room
	I put on headphones to drown them out

Karate Chop: Even though they are fighting and I slam the door of my room, I still love and accept myself.
Karate Chop: Even though they're fighting and I'm trying to drown them out, I'd rather feel safe and calm.

Eyebrow: They're fighting again . . .
Side of Eye: I slam my bedroom door . . .
Under Eye: They're still fighting . . .
Under Nose: I put on my headphones . . .
Chin: I can still hear them . . .

Collarbone: They're fighting . . .
Under Arm: I'm trying to drown them out . . .
Top of Head: My parents are always fighting.

Once we tapped on Kayla's actions, we were able to uncover some of her thoughts and feelings about their fighting and then tap on those. You know by now how much better you feel after tapping on your own thoughts and feelings, so try this yourself: tap on your actions, then see what thoughts and feelings start to emerge to fill in the blanks. Make a note of them in your notebook and use your notes to create setup statements. Then tap away!

Here's how this step looked for Kayla:

Event	Thought	Feeling	Action
Something happens	You have a thought	That creates a feeling	You do something
Parents are fighting	I think they're going to divorce	I feel scared	I turn up the headphones
	They don't care that it upsets me	I feel angry	I slam the door
	Is it my fault?	I feel sad	I burst into tears

Karate Chop: Even though I feel sad when they fight, I love and accept myself.
Karate Chop: Even though I also feel afraid when they fight, I love and accept myself.
Karate Chop: Even though their fighting makes me so angry, I love and accept myself.

Eyebrow: They're fighting a lot lately . . .
Side of Eye: I feel sad when I hear them fight . . .
Under Eye: I just want them to be happy . . .
Under Nose: When they raise their voices, I feel sad . . .
Chin: What if they break up . . .
Collarbone: I don't know what I'd do . . .
Under Arm: Right now, I'll acknowledge the sadness . . .
Top of Head: It's okay to tell them how fighting affects me.

How are you doing as you tap along with Kayla's phrases? Kayla tapped some of these phrases almost every day when her parents' arguing was really intense. It's okay to tap about this as much as you need to.

One day she said she was worried that it was her fault they were fighting. Of course we talked about the fact that it *wasn't* her fault that her parents were having problems, but lots of kids feel this way, so it's an important thing to tap on.

Karate Chop: Even though my parents are fighting again, and I think it must be my fault . . .

Karate Chop: Even though their fighting affects me, it's their choice and it's not my fault.

Karate Chop: Even though they're fighting, I remind myself that right now I'm okay.

Eyebrow: They're fighting . . . .
Side of Eye: I wonder if it's my fault . . .
Under Eye: But they're choosing to fight . . .
Under Nose: It's their choice . . .
Chin: It affects me . . .
Collarbone: But it's not my fault . . .
Under Arm: I'll be okay . . .
Top of Head: Right now, I'm okay . . .

Using the phrase "Right now I'm okay" is a great way to keep your thoughts and feelings more neutral instead of jumping forward into the world of worries and what-ifs.

What if . . .

If you have a friend whose parents have gone through a divorce, I'm sure you've heard that it can be super stressful. So, it's normal to wonder sometimes what would happen if your parents did the same thing. And so if your parents are arguing, you might jump pretty quickly to worrying, *What if they split up and divorce?*

The what-ifs are useful if you're packing for a trip and wondering, *What if it rains?* Then you plan ahead and pack a raincoat. But when you're listening to your parents argue again, jumping ahead to *What if they divorce?* does you no good. It only adds to your stress, which is already accelerated because they're arguing.

Event	Thought	Feeling	Action
Something happens	You have a thought	That creates a feeling	You do something
They argue	What if they divorce?	I feel afraid, nervous	I keep thinking about it
	What if we move away?	I feel anxious	I get tense
	What if . . . ?	I feel overwhelmed	I tap!

I want you to practice interrupting any what-ifs that jump into your mind. Grab them as soon as you notice them. When you allow the what-ifs, you can see how quickly your thoughts and worries can spiral from *My parents are arguing* to imagining yourself living in a different country with a wicked stepmother and evil stepsisters. But it's important to remember that even though they're arguing, right now everything is okay. I know it might not feel okay, but tapping can help you realize that it is. Practice it as often and as long as you think of the dreaded what-ifs.

First, get out your notebook and write down the awful what-ifs taking up space in your mind and in your stress backpack. This will get them out of your head, and then you'll be able to see them and create setup statements with them.

What if:
They get a divorce . . . Right now everything's okay.
They end up hating each other . . . Right now everything's okay.
They hurt each other . . . Right now everything's okay.
We never have another family holiday . . . Right now everything's okay.
I have to move away from my friends . . . Right now everything's okay.
I never see my BFF again . . . Right now everything's okay.
I have to change schools . . . Right now everything's okay.
I have to start all over . . . Right now everything's okay.
I never see my parent again . . . Right now everything's okay.
We end up being broke . . . Right now everything's okay.
What if it's my fault . . . ? Right now everything's okay. (P.S. It's not your fault!)

You can simply tap all the points while going over this list and your own list of what-ifs. Notice whether one or two what-ifs have a bigger level of intensity and then create setup statements with those; do full rounds of tapping with reminder phrases. Always finish tapping on what-ifs by repeating the statement "Right now everything's okay."

Eyebrow: What if they get a divorce . . .
Side of Eye: Right now everything's okay . . .
Under Eye: What if they get a divorce . . .
Under Nose: Right now everything's okay.
Chin: What if they get a divorce . . .
Collarbone: Right now everything's okay.
Under Arm: What if they get a divorce . . .
Top of Head: Right now everything's okay.

There's More to Explore

I wanted to get you started here in this chapter on tapping about your parents' relationship, but there's lots more to explore on this topic. In "There's More to Explore" I've shared a bunch more of my work with Kayla for you to tap along with. And if you're wondering how Kayla's doing, she's doing great! Here's what she asked me to share with you:

> *Okay, girls, I totally get how awful and stressful it is when your parents are fighting. I went through it and I couldn't stand it, but you need to know that you're not alone and that this wild tapping stuff really helps! My parents were so wrapped up in themselves (sorry, Mom and Dad, but you were) that they didn't even really notice how freaked out I was getting. I'm just glad that I got to do this tapping with Christine. It really saved my sanity over the year of all this messed-up stuff that was happening with my parents. Sometimes it felt like my world was crumbling around me, and on top of it, there were times when I felt like I had to protect my mom from finding out what was going on with my dad. So please go through and tap on all the stuff I tapped on, even if your family stuff happened ages ago. It's hard to explain, but when I did the tapping, I calmed down almost immediately about the specific stuff that was happening. I was able to see how it all affected me, and don't get me started on the stepfamily stuff . . . tap tap tap.*

In a weird way, it was almost like I was able to observe what was happening and know that it wasn't my fault—I would always be safe and things really would end up being okay. And they are. I still use tapping all the time (you will too!) and, at 17 years old, I feel like a pretty normal teenage girl. I love being aware of, and in charge of, my own thoughts, feelings, and actions even if my parents are creating crazy events for me to deal with!

TAPFIRMATION
I'd rather feel calm and comfortable despite the chaos at home.

Chapter 8

TAPPING ABOUT YOUR RELATIONSHIPS WITH PARENTS AND FAMILY

Madeline's mother was super strict, but at 15 Madeline wanted to do things with her friends. It seemed like her mother was always saying no and Madeline was doing a lot of crying, yelling, and door slamming in response. It didn't make sense that she wasn't allowed to do things with her three best friends, whose parents always said yes to activities and adventures.

I was showing Madeline some tapping exercises and the big thing she wanted to tap on was her mother saying no all the time. I asked her about her thoughts and feelings when her mother said no. She felt frustrated, angry, and hopeless.

In this chapter, I'm going to share with you the tapping I did with Madeline about this conflict with her mother, because I know it's something that many teenage girls can relate to. What Madeline really wanted was to tap on her mother to make her say yes, but we came up with other solutions.

. . . .

CASSIDY'S COMMENT

When you feel like your parents are challenging or ignoring your choices, your opinions, and your need for independence, it can feel pretty harsh. But here's what's great about tapping on these conflicts that you might be having with your parents: instead of just reacting, you start paying attention to your thoughts and feelings. Why is that so great? Because when you're aware of your thoughts and feelings, it helps you communicate your wants, needs, and opinions more clearly to the adults in your life. And we know from experience that clear, calm communication can lead to getting more of what you want! Right?

As you go through these tapping exercises, you'll see how sometimes we seem like a series of reactions to stuff our parents say or do. No judgment, it's normal. But when we tap on the thoughts and feelings we're having, we get calmer and clearer, and we are able to communicate better instead of just having a big reaction that ends the conversations. When there's more conversation, often there's more negotiation, and more chance of situations turning out in your favor. Tapping really can be a secret weapon!

. . . .

Your parents are used to being in charge of you

From the moment you were born, your parents have been making decisions for you. They've been in charge of keeping you safe, warm, fed, clothed, and happy. They arranged playdates for you, chose kids for you to play with, and canceled playdates with kids they thought were bullies. If you weren't with a parent, you were either in school, in an activity, or with a designated caregiver. They knew where you were and what you were doing all the time. So your parents are used to being 100 percent in charge of you.

As you get older, you're choosing your own friends, arranging your own social life, picking your own clothes, and so on. You might crave more independence and want to make your own decisions about your hair, makeup, and so on. You're figuring out who you are, what you like, and who you want to be. You're not a kid anymore, though sometimes you might feel as if you're being treated like a child, and maybe you're even being told to stop acting like a child. At the same time, you're not an adult either, and while you might be longing to be grown up, you're still dependent on your parents to take care of you. Deep down, you really want them to be there for you and to have your back. But sometimes you want them to leave you to do your own thing, and it can be hard to find that balance.

As you go through this complex process, conflicts may arise with your parents, who are not only used to taking complete charge of your well-being, they're invested in wanting the best for you as you become your awesome self. They might have opinions about whom you hang out with and what clothes you wear, and they might not want you to go out with friends on a school night. These sorts of things might result in day-to-day conflicts. And there can be bigger conflicts as well. I'm going to give you some tapping solutions for helping you feel more calm, confident, and powerful as you face them.

Madeline's mother kept saying no!

This is the perfect issue to practice using your Event-Thought-Feeling-Action chart to create tapping statements. Madeline's letting us use her chart as an example. I told you already that she had really strong reactions to her mom's saying no. Madeline's father wasn't around and so she felt stuck with her mom, who didn't want her to have a life.

Madeline did all this tapping and eventually was able to talk to her mom about her thoughts and feelings, instead of just reacting. She'll tell you about that in a bit. Right now, please tap along, and see if you feel a bit better.

Event	Thought	Feeling	Action
Something happens	You have a thought	That creates a feeling	You do something
They won't let me do anything	They don't trust me	I feel angry	I shut down
They automatically say no!	They're treating me like a kid	I feel frustrated	I start yelling
	It's not fair	I feel hopeless	I cry

Karate Chop: Even though they won't let me do that thing, so I think they don't trust me, I love and accept myself.
Karate Chop: Even though they're treating me like a kid, I love and accept myself.
Karate Chop: Even though I start yelling when they say no, I love and accept myself.
Karate Chop: Even though I feel so angry and frustrated, I love and accept myself.

Karate Chop: Even though when they won't let me do something I shut down, I'd rather feel calmer.

Karate Chop: Even though it's not fair that I can't do that, I still love and accept myself.

Karate Chop: Even though I feel so hopeless, I love and accept myself.

Eyebrow:	They won't let me do anything . . .
Side of Eye:	They don't trust me . . .
Under Eye:	They treat me like a kid . . .
Under Nose:	I just start yelling . . .
Chin:	I'm so angry . . .
Collarbone:	I'm so frustrated . . .
Under Arm:	I just shut down . . .
Top of Head:	I feel so hopeless . . .

Eyebrow:	It's not fair . . .
Side of Eye:	I can't believe it . . .
Under Eye:	I'd rather feel calmer . . .
Under Nose:	I want what I want . . .
Chin:	But they're in charge . . .
Collarbone:	But I'm in charge of my reaction . . .
Under Arm:	I'd rather be calmer . . .
Top of Head:	I'd rather be calm.

Tip from Cassidy: Tap While Arguing

Having conflict with your parents is normal, but it's also really stressful. If you're having a conversation/argument with your mom or dad and you're both getting more and more upset, here's a good trick: both of you tap while you're talking. It's best if you start a discussion with both of you tapping. If you're already getting into it, try and remember to stop for a second and start tapping, and hopefully your parent will follow your lead.

Sometimes in a big, heated argument it is hard to stop everything and say, "Hey, Dad, let's stop and tap on our faces!" If this is the case, just keep tapping yourself, whether it's the Butterfly Hug, the finger points, or the tapping points. You will feel calmer and more present, and you might even win! My mom and I tap a lot together so we're used to it, and sometimes we just burst out laughing. It's worth practicing and playing with it to see how you feel.

"No matter what I do, it isn't good enough"

Alyssa was so excited when she got her senior project back and found she got an A. She'd worked really hard on it, and she felt really proud of the project when she handed it in to her teacher. So getting an A meant a lot to her and she knew she'd earned it. She couldn't wait to tell her dad, thinking for sure he'd be proud of her.

Imagine how devastated she felt when all her father said to her was, "Why didn't you get A-plus?" Alyssa told me, "He might as well have punched me in the stomach. I couldn't speak, I couldn't answer, and I just left the room."

So many people have a story about an accomplishment that they were super excited about until their parents said something to them that felt diminishing and devastating. I have several of my own stories from my teenage years, so I know how the hurt from the past can affect how you feel about yourself in the future. I really want you to take your time and tap on these issues now. I don't want you to take this hurt with you into adulthood.

If you've ever felt like what you do isn't good enough, I've put together a lot of setup statements for you below. You can tap on all of them or pick the ones that really ring true for you.

Karate Chop: Even though I got an A on my exam and my parent asked why it wasn't A+, I love and accept myself.

Karate Chop: Even though I came in second and they asked me why I didn't come in first, I love and accept myself.

Karate Chop: Even though I feel so frustrated trying to please them, I love and respect myself.

Karate Chop: Even though I felt devastated, I know I did my best, and I love and accept myself and I'm proud of myself.

Karate Chop: Even though I feel like I can't do anything right, I love and accept myself.

Karate Chop: Even though I feel so tense about doing well, I'd rather feel calmer.

Karate Chop: Even though they won't give me credit for my accomplishments, I love and accept myself.

Karate Chop: Even though I feel like I'm never good enough, I'd rather love and accept myself.

Eyebrow: Even an A isn't good enough for them . . .
Side of Eye: I think I'm doing my best . . .
Under Eye: But when that's not good enough . . .
Under Nose: I don't know what else to do . . .
Chin: I feel so frustrated . . .
Collarbone: I feel so tense . . .
Under Arm: I'm looking for their approval . . .
Top of Head: I'm afraid I'll never get it . . .

Eyebrow: I thought I did so well . . .
Side of Eye: They thought I should do better . . .
Under Eye: I was happy with my grade . . .
Under Nose: But now I feel devastated . . .
Chin: I know I did my best . . .
Collarbone: Why are they so hard to please . . .
Under Arm: I'd rather be calmer and confident . . .
Top of Head: I'd rather be pleased with my accomplishments.

Alyssa felt much calmer after tapping on this complex issue. Not only did she go back to being excited about getting an A on the project, she was also able to calm her anxiety about doing well enough to please her very critical father.

I also made a suggestion to Alyssa that may help you if you have a critical parent who's not very good at giving you positive feedback and reinforcement for the work you do. Try making a list of the positive things other people—teachers, trusted adults, and friends—have said about your accomplishments. You might even bring out a report card that you're happy with.

Then tap on all the tapping points while you're reading the list of things people have said, and the positive comments on your report card. This way, your mind gets to take in some positive reinforcement. I know it's not the same as hearing that your parent is proud of you, but it might help to take the edge off the pain. It's a great exercise just to collect these positive remarks in a notebook that you can keep adding to and reading if you've had a rough day. Then you can tap while reading your collection!

Alyssa wrote to me later:

Thank you so much for tapping with me about my father making that comment about only getting an A on my project. I realize that I might never impress him, but the exercise you gave me helped me pay attention to the positive things that other people say to me. I'd rather keep paying attention to those things instead of just focusing on the words of my critical father. I work hard and I do my best and I want to feel happy about that and proud of myself. I know that the pressure I've felt to be the best at everything was coming from him and that it's okay for me to relax and still do my best for me.

There's More to Explore

Madeline did a lot of tapping on her conflict with her parents, and if you want to tap along even more on the things that popped up for her, I know you'll get some real relief. You can pop to page 197 in the back of the book and tap on more topics.

TAPFIRMATION

Everyone's doing the best they can with the information they have.

Chapter 9

TAPPING ABOUT YOUR SIBLINGS AND CONFLICTS

Lots of teenage girls have kind, loving, and close relationships with their siblings, and lots don't. Even though you're in the same family with the same parents, you may have very different personalities, characteristics, and behaviors. If you're living with stepsiblings, you may feel super connected to them or you may be experiencing some conflict at home. It's so important for you to do tapping on these issues because you have the right to feel at home in your home. If your sibling discord is feeling like bullying, check out Chapter 12, where I talk and tap about bullying. Hopefully this tapping will give you some relief and maybe some insight into what you can do about the conflicts.

. . . .

CASSIDY'S COMMENT

I think it's normal to fight with your brothers or sisters. But what really bugs girls about their siblings is being compared to them! Who wants to hear that your sister is smarter than you, or your brother is a superstar? You're busy being yourself, but people want you to be like your sibling. So frustrating. If this is your world, do this tapping right now.

. . . .

Alexis was quieter than her sister, and not as social

Alexis was quieter than her older sister, Elizabeth. She liked being around people, but it took a lot of her energy, so she needed time alone to recharge. Her inner world was super rich and she really enjoyed her own company, often doing something creative. She had some select friends whom she shared things with privately, but she wasn't interested in, or comfortable with, being part of a big group.

Usually, Alexis was comfortable with herself and her quietness but when she entered tenth grade, she had a teacher who had been a big fan of her sister and expected Alexis to have the same temperament. One day the teacher said to Alexis, "Are you sure you're Elizabeth's sister? You are nothing like her. She's so friendly and outgoing, and she always participated in class discussions. I thought you'd be more like her. Boy, was I wrong." The teacher kind of laughed while she was saying this, but you can imagine how upset Alexis was. For her, there was no humor in the teacher's comment. She just walked away from the teacher without saying anything, went into the girls' bathroom, and burst into tears.

It wasn't unusual for Alexis to be compared to Elizabeth, her outgoing, talkative, sometimes loud, expressive sister. She'd been called the shy one, or the quiet one, and it had sometimes bothered her—but when the teacher spelled it out the way she did, it hit Alexis that people actually preferred her sister. She thought, *People like Elizabeth more, she's better than me.* Then she started to remember all the hurtful things people had said to her over the years, the worst being "I guess your sister got all the personality."

If this feels familiar to you at all, please follow the tapping below. This tapping helped Alexis to see her own positive qualities, to accept that she was different from her sister and awesome in her own unique way. I'm going to supply lots of setup statements for you, so please tap along with as many as you feel apply to you.

Karate Chop: "Even though the teacher said my sister was a better person than me, I love and accept myself."
Karate Chop: "Even though someone said my sister got all the personality, I have my own unique personality."
Karate Chop: "Even though people compare me to my sister, I love and accept myself the way I am."
Karate Chop: "Even though I feel less than my sister when they compare us, I love and accept myself."

Karate Chop: "Even though they say outright that they prefer her, I still love and accept myself."

Karate Chop: "Even though sometimes I feel like I should be more like her, I'm going to be me."

Karate Chop: "Even though I love my sister, I am not my sister, and I love and accept myself the way I am."

Karate Chop: "Even though sometimes people say stupid, hurtful things, I love and accept myself."

Karate Chop: "Even though my sister is awesome, I am also awesome."

Eyebrow: I'm different from my sister . . .
Side of Eye: But it seems like people like her better . . .
Under Eye: And think she's more fun . . .
Under Nose: Why can't they just appreciate me . . .
Chin: I'm tired of being compared . . .
Collarbone: I have a lot of good qualities . . .
Under Arm: But people seem to favor the extrovert . . .
Top of Head: I'd rather feel comfortable being me . . .

Eyebrow: I can't believe the stupid things people say . . .
Side of Eye: Don't they see how hurtful they are . . .
Under Eye: I'm quieter than my sister . . .
Under Nose: I feel inferior . . .
Chin: I'd rather feel awesome . . .
Collarbone: I think people want me to be like her . . .
Under Arm: But I can't be like her . . .
Top of Head: I'm too busy being me . . .

Eyebrow: I love my sister . . .
Side of Eye: I am not my sister . . .
Under Eye: She is outgoing and awesome . . .
Under Nose: I prefer to go inside to get my energy . . .
Chin: She's outgoing, I'm ingoing . . .
Collarbone: And I love and accept myself this way . . .
Under Arm: This is the way I am and I'm awesome . . .
Top of Head: I am uniquely me.

It can feel like a big deal if you're being compared to a sister or a brother in a way that leaves you feeling less-than. Rather than ignore the feeling, I'd like you take the time to tap on it.

"My sibling has challenges and I get put aside"

If you have a sibling who has special needs or health issues and needs more attention from your parents and others than you yourself get, you might have some feelings about that. Please don't judge your feelings; just know that your feelings are real. Hopefully some tapping will give you a bit more peace.

Karate Chop: Even though my parents always put my sibling first, I love and accept myself.

Karate Chop: Even though my sibling needs more from my parents, so they get more attention, I love and accept myself.

Karate Chop: Even though it's hard because I feel like I need more attention, I love and accept myself.

Karate Chop: Even though sometimes I wish I had something wrong with me so I'd get more attention, I'm going to remain healthy.

Karate Chop: Even though sometimes I feel guilty because I am healthy, it's okay to be healthy.

Karate Chop: Even though sometimes I hate my sibling because they're so needy, I want to love and accept myself and my sibling.

Karate Chop: Even though I feel guilty because I resent my sibling, I acknowledge my complex feelings and I love and accept myself.

Eyebrow: They always put my sibling first . . .
Side of Eye: My sibling needs so much attention . . .
Under Eye: They're so needy . . .
Under Nose: Sometimes I resent them for being so needy . . .
Chin: I feel guilty that I resent them . . .
Collarbone: Sometimes I even hate them . . .
Under Arm: And I feel guilty about that . . .
Top of Head: I'd rather be more peaceful . . .

Eyebrow: Sometimes I just want to say . . .
Side of Eye: What about me? . . .
Under Eye: Parents are so attentive to my sibling . . .
Under Nose: What about me . . .
Chin: Sometimes I wish I was sick too . . .
Collarbone: Then I'd get more attention . . .
Under Arm: But I am well . . .
Top of Head: I'm going to stay healthy.

Remember that any of these statements and phrases can be turned into an entire setup statement and round of tapping. For example, if you've identified with the idea of sometimes wishing you'd get sick, that is a really good thing to tap on.

Karate Chop: Even though sometimes I wish I were ill so I could get more attention, I love and accept myself anyway.
Karate Chop: Even though I sometimes wish I could get sick and get all this attention away from my sibling, I know I would rather be healthy.
Karate Chop: Even though sometimes I envy my sick sibling, I am grateful to be healthy.

Eyebrow: Sometimes I wish I'd get sick . . .
Side of Eye: To get more attention . . .
Under Eye: I'm tired of being ignored . . .
Under Nose: Because I'm healthy . . .
Chin: "But I'm grateful to be healthy . . .
Collarbone: I am choosing health . . .
Under Arm: And I'm open to finding healthy ways . . .
Top of Head: To get the attention I need.

Always remember that you can keep going back to tap on anything, anytime. You're growing, changing, and evolving, and it makes sense that you may still be bothered about things you've already tapped on. Be easy on yourself about it.

Now we're going to head into another chapter that will help you deal with some of the things that might be happening at school. Keep tapping!

There's More to Explore

There's more tapping for you to do if you have conflicts with siblings. Just turn to page 199.

TAPFIRMATION

I'd rather feel peaceful with my people.

part four

TAPPING ON STUFF THAT HAPPENS AT SCHOOL

. . . .

CASSIDY'S COMMENT

How are you doing with your tapping? It's pretty amazing, isn't it? You can take charge of how you're feeling in stressful situations and come up with new ways to solve problems in all areas of your life. It's almost like you have some sort of magical power that no one knows about. I've loved having this secret weapon of tapping and now you get to use it too! And the great thing is that no matter what part of your life is the most challenging, you can use tapping there too.

The next section is all about tapping for stuff that's happening at school. And whether you like school or not, we have to go and so it makes up a massive part of our lives. And it's different for everybody. Maybe you like the academic part of school but get stressed about the social part. It might be the other way around for you. I know lots of girls who are super social and school is the center of their social life, and they never want to miss a day—but they really struggle with certain subjects.

Whatever your experience with school, there is something for you in this part of the book. I've calmed my own stress about certain exams with tapping and as I write this, I'm heading into my senior year and planning for college next year. So I'm definitely going to do some tapping and let you read this part of the book!

. . . .

Chapter 10

TAPPING ABOUT SCHOOLWORK

Remember I talked about that big stress survey at the beginning of the book? Most of the teenagers in the survey, in fact 83 percent of them, said school was a big source of stress in their lives. That means that even if you like school and are doing well and getting good grades, school is still stressful!

. . . .

CASSIDY'S COMMENT

Have you ever had your mind go blank and completely bombed an exam, even though you'd studied like mad for the last two weeks? I have! Before I started tapping I would get so nervous before a test that I wouldn't be able to concentrate. It was like I'd never seen those words before. All the thoughts, feelings, and sensations in the Even Though list you'll find on the next page? That was all me.

One day we had an exam and the teacher put the test paper on my desk, and I just started taking the test. I was halfway through, kind of breezing through actually, when I realized what I was doing. I was taking the exam. Not a speck of freezing. Tapping is my antifreeze!

Seriously, do these tapping exercises and rock your exams!

. . . .

Test anxiety!

The pressure is on! You've got a quiz, test, or exam in your future and you're freaking out. Take a minute to look at your thoughts and feelings about tests and exams. Grab your notebook and write things down as they come to mind. Here's a list of typical things that girls have reported when they see a test looming before them. Are you feeling any of these?

Remember that just adding "Even though" and "I love and accept myself" creates a perfect setup statement, and you can tap on any and all of these statements that apply to you. Before you start tapping, check your level of intensity and see, on a scale of 0 to 10, how you're feeling right now as you think about your upcoming test.

I'm not prepared . . .

I can't breathe . . .

I can't focus . . .

I can't study . . .

I feel sick . . .

I'm going to fail . . .

I'm not ready . . .

My heart is racing . . .

I feel so anxious . . .

I can't think . . .

I can't remember anything . . .

I'm afraid I might freeze . . .

I'm afraid I might fail . . .

I don't understand _____.

I'm not good at _____.

I love and accept myself.

Now, I want you to write down what you'd rather think and feel when writing exams. As you do this, notice if you start to feel calmer. Here are some phrases to get you started. Have fun with it and allow yourself to do some creative thinking.

- I'd rather be calm and confident . . .

- I'd rather be focused and alert . . .

- I'd rather be an exam wizard . . .

- I'd rather be stress-free . . .

- I'd rather have access to all the information I've collected . . .

- I'd rather imagine my pen is a wand . . .

- I'd rather have all the info at my fingertips . . .

These are all great nuggets to create setup statements. You can mix and match these along with your own ideas, thoughts, and feelings about tests and exams.

Karate Chop: Even though I'm not prepared, I'd rather be calm and confident.
Karate Chop: Even though my stomach has butterflies, I'd rather be stress-free.
Karate Chop: Even though I'm afraid I'm not ready, I'd rather have access to everything I've studied.

Eyebrow: I'm not prepared . . .
Side of Eye: But I'd rather be calm and confident . . .
Under Eye: I have butterflies in my stomach . . .
Under Nose: I'd rather be stress free . . .
Chin: I'm afraid I'm not ready . . .
Collarbone: I'd rather have all the info at my fingertips . . .
Under Arm: I'd rather trust my mind . . .
Top of Head: And trust myself . . .

Eyebrow: I'm taking deep breaths . . .
Side of Eye: I'm releasing this nervous feeling . . .
Under Eye: I'll probably do okay on this test . . .
Under Nose: What if I do great . . .
Chin: It's possible that I'll do really well . . .
Collarbone: I'd rather be calm and confident . . .
Under Arm: I'd rather access all my knowledge . . .
Top of Head: Easily and effortlessly.

After tapping, check your level of intensity again. If you're still feeling anxious, tap again and even choose a few different tapping targets to address different aspects of your anxiety.

Test-Taking Tip

A great trick to help you study and get more focused is to do the Butterfly Hug (page 26). This helps balance your left brain and right brain and helps them work together. It's like it helps you access all the files that the information is stored in. Also, it helps to calm you down in general. I suggest doing the Butterfly Hug before you sit down to study or do homework or anything that requires your concentration.

Olivia was the queen of avoiding homework

Olivia was in ninth grade and avoided studying and homework like the plague. Her parents were getting concerned about her being able to handle high school. They tried eliminating her distractions, taking away her phone for several hours a day (sound familiar?), but she still had to use the computer to do homework and she'd get distracted online.

As her parents got angrier with her, Olivia got more stuck. They arranged for her to see her school counselor, who did some tapping with her. They did some basic tapping, mostly leaving out the thoughts and feelings and focusing on the facts of what was happening. They started with the simple phrase: "I get distracted." That was their first tapping target. Her level of intensity was at 10 out of 10.

Here's what Olivia tapped on. Tap along and see what you notice for yourself. As some girls have reported, you might be able to focus on your homework and studying by tapping a few rounds of this idea. Or, like Olivia, you might have some more tapping to do. But start here:

"I get distracted"

Karate Chop: Even though I'm getting distracted by social media, I love and accept myself.

Karate Chop: Even though I'm getting distracted by _____, I love and accept myself.

Karate Chop: Even though I'm allowing myself to get distracted, I'd rather focus on my work.

Karate Chop: Even though I'm distracted, I have the power to focus on the work I have to do.

Eyebrow: I'm distracted so easily . . .
Side of Eye: I need to check everything . . .
Under Eye: I know I'm allowing myself . . .
Under Nose: To get distracted . . .
Chin: The distractions don't have power over me . . .
Collarbone: I am in charge . . .
Under Arm: I have the power to focus . . .
Top of Head: I'm going to focus . . .

Eyebrow: I'd rather be on social media . . .
Side of Eye: But my work is more important . . .
Under Eye: I'm afraid I'll miss something . . .
Under Nose: But I'd rather not miss out on school . . .
Chin: I'm in charge of where my attention goes . . .
Collarbone: I'm going to focus on my homework . . .
Under Arm: I'm going to give my attention to studying . . .
Top of Head: I have power over my distractions.

Olivia did feel a bit better, but her level of intensity only dropped to 7 out of 10. As she tapped, she realized that there was more going on than her being distracted, like there was a missing piece to the puzzle. When the school counselor asked her what felt so stressful about doing homework, Olivia said, "I don't want to do the homework because I'm afraid it won't be perfect." They tapped on that.

"I'm afraid it won't be perfect"

Olivia and her school counselor realized that if she avoided homework and studying, then if she did poorly in school—if everything wasn't perfect—it was because she hadn't prepared and not because *she* was imperfect.

Maybe you know that doing things perfectly is a big deal for you. Or maybe you don't think it really applies to you. But please do this tapping that Olivia did anyway. If the desire to be perfect is lurking in the background—and for many girls it is—tapping will help resolve this for you.

Karate Chop: Even though I put off doing homework because I'm afraid it won't be perfect, I love and accept myself.
Karate Chop: Even though I put it off because I know it won't be perfect, I am doing the best I can.
Karate Chop: Even though I'm afraid of making mistakes and not being perfect, I'm still going to do my best.

Eyebrow: I don't want to do it . . .
Side of Eye: If it's not going to be perfect . . .
Under Eye: So I keep putting it off . . .
Under Nose: I give myself permission . . .
Chin: To be imperfect . . .
Collarbone: It's okay to make mistakes . . .
Under Arm: I'm doing my best . . .
Top of Head: And will keep doing my best.

Are you wondering how this worked out for Olivia? Here's what she wanted me to share with you:

My parents asked how my meeting with the counselor went and I told them it seemed okay, but I didn't tell them about the tapping. So my parents were shocked that I announced after dinner that I was going to my room to do my homework. I always had to keep the door of my room open and they would lurk outside to see if I was on social media or doing my nails instead of my homework. In one night they would usually interrupt me five times. This night they didn't come in once, and this time I was the one who was shocked! I did all my homework in a couple of hours instead of the four hours it would normally take me. Now I'm telling all my friends to tap and I'm thinking of setting up a tapping club at school!

There's More to Explore

Olivia did a bunch of really helpful tapping and wanted to share everything she tapped on with other girls who have different reasons for avoiding homework. Hop over to page 202 for some other things you can tap on.

TAPFIRMATION
When school feels overwhelming, I'll take one piece at a time.

Chapter 11

TAPPING ABOUT GRADES AND REPORT CARDS

Some parents, teachers, and caregivers put a ton of pressure on teenage girls to get good grades and others are happy to leave it in the girls' hands. If you're in the former group, it can be very stressful to deal with the pressure others impose. And pressure from family and parents can be different from the pressure you might feel from a teacher. You may really want to please a teacher who thinks you can accomplish more than you're doing, whereas you might feel annoyed about the pressure you feel from your parents. Or vice versa!

It's also stressful to deal with the pressure you might be putting on *yourself* to do well. I'm sharing a story with you about Madison, who was putting lots of pressure on herself about her grades. You'll be able to use the same setup statements she used for your own situation, no matter where your pressure about your grades is coming from.

. . . .

CASSIDY'S COMMENT

Congratulations! You graduated from the previous chapter about getting homework and assignments done. But you might also be graduating into stress about getting good grades and planning to get into colleges. When I was in elementary school I sometimes had a hard time getting homework done. Now in high school, I'm fine with finishing assignments without too much procrastination and distraction (thank you, tapping). But I am stressed out about getting good grades! Who isn't? When I'm worried about my grades, I get stressed out, and because I get stressed out, I can't focus and therefore get bad grades, which gives me more stress. It's this terrible cycle that is hard to stop. But when I tap on the worrying, I focus better, get better grades, and stop the cycle. I have seen a lot of girls worrying about grades because their parents get involved and stressed, which leads to more stress. So if that sounds familiar, this will be a great chapter for you.

. . . .

Madison was worried about getting good grades

Madison did well in school and knew that she eventually wanted to study sciences in college and maybe go on to become a doctor. She'd had a plan since tenth grade and worked hard to stay near the top of her class. She had always known that she was headed for college, and she was pretty confident that she would win scholarships, get into the college she wanted, and eventually achieve her dream. She also felt very fortunate that her parents had been saving money so that she could pay for her education.

But as she was starting her senior year and settling into her classes, her father lost his job. Her parents were both stressed and it seemed to Madison like they were scrambling to take care of things financially. Madison wanted to ask about her college fund, but she felt selfish thinking about herself when her parents were so stressed.

Instead of talking with her parents about her concerns, Madison felt like she had to come up with a plan herself to make sure that her college aspirations were secure. She decided that she had better work even harder than she already did so that she would be sure to win scholarships.

Now it wasn't a bad plan, but Madison became so worried about getting even better grades than before that the stress started interfering with her ability to do her work. She was getting headaches and wasn't sleeping well. Subjects that had been easy for her before became more difficult and she felt like she was losing her edge. She was beginning to think that she'd never even get into college, let alone get scholarships. She wanted help before her grades suffered.

Madison and I did some creative tapping together to help her sort out what was happening. Madison's level of intensity regarding her worry about her grades was at a 10 out of 10 and we started tapping on the karate chop point while saying these setup statements:

Karate Chop: Even though I'm worried about my grades, I love and accept myself.
Karate Chop: Even though it's hard for me to concentrate, I'm doing my best.
Karate Chop: Even though my parents are stressed about money, I'd rather be calmer.

Eyebrow:	I'm worried about my grades . . .
Side of Eye:	What if I fail . . .
Under Eye:	My parents are stressed and so am I . . .
Under Nose:	It's hard to concentrate . . .
Chin:	I've never been worried about school before . . .
Collarbone:	I am doing my best . . .
Under Arm:	But I'm so stressed . . .
Top of Head:	I'd rather feel calmer.

When Madison took a deep breath and checked in with her level of intensity, it had moved from 10 out of 10 to 6 out of 10. With her head feeling a bit clearer, she said she realized she didn't actually know the status of her college fund. She'd assumed her parents would have to use it since her dad lost his job.

Karate Chop: Even though I don't know the facts about my college fund, I love and accept myself.
Karate Chop: Even though I assumed the worst-case scenario, it might not be that bad.
Karate Chop: Even though I'm stressing about something I don't understand, I'd rather get all the info.

Eyebrow:	I don't have all the facts . . .
Side of Eye:	But I'm stressing anyway . . .
Under Eye:	I assumed the worst about this . . .
Under Nose:	They wouldn't want me to stress out too much . . .
Chin:	Maybe I'll just ask them . . .
Collarbone:	It's okay to ask my parents about it . . .
Under Arm:	I'd rather focus on doing my best . . .
Top of Head:	Instead of preparing for the worst.

You can see that while tapping, Madison went from feeling very stressed and anxious about her grades to coming up with a solution on her own. In the end, her story turned out well. She spoke to her parents about her concern and they assured her that her college fund was intact and she had nothing to worry about. The tapping had reduced her stress about her grades in general, and she had her best semester ever and was on her way to winning scholarships anyway!

Madison's is an interesting example because you can see that she was worrying about something without having all the information—which is so easy to do! The pressure and stress she was experiencing came from her *thinking* there was a problem. Tapping helped her to see that she was operating without having the right info, creating a worst-case scenario and caught up in negative what-ifs, trying to solve a problem that might not exist. And of course, even if that worst-case scenario had turned out to be the reality, tapping would have helped her find her way through it.

· ·

CASSIDY'S COMMENT

I've known girls who were afraid of getting into serious trouble if they didn't do well on exams. Their parents were not happy if they slacked off at all, and if their grades started slipping, their parents would impose harsh punishments. I showed tapping to a friend I was studying with because she was getting freaked out from the pressure. Because studying stressed her out so much, she didn't want to study at all. After I showed her the technique, she instantly stopped freaking out and went back to studying. She did really well on her exams and got her confidence back.

· ·

"I'm in trouble if I don't do well!"

While some parents are understanding of challenges in school, others take a harder line. If you think you're going to make your parents angry if you get a poor grade or they'll ground you if you fail a test, you may be creating a worst-case scenario or you may actually be right! Either way, tapping can help you cope with the stress.

Karate Chop: Even though I'll be in trouble if I don't do well, and I feel so much pressure, I love and accept myself.
Karate Chop: Even though I won't be able to do _____ if I don't get an A, I'd rather feel calm and peaceful.

Karate Chop: Even though my parents will freak if I get a low grade, I'm trying to stay calm.

Eyebrow: I'll get punished if I don't do well . . .
Side of Eye: I will lose a benefit if I don't get an A . . .
Under Eye: I won't be able to do things I want . . .
Under Nose: So much pressure . . .
Chin: I can't concentrate because of this pressure . . .
Collarbone: They will freak out . . .
Under Arm: I'd rather feel calm . . .
Top of Head: I'd rather calmly do my best.

What are you saying to yourself about your grades?

The stuff you say to yourself in the privacy of your own mind is really important to pay attention to. It's called *self-talk*. When you get your report card, what are you saying to yourself about it? Here are some possibilities. As you read these, notice how you feel.

- Oh, I didn't do as well as I thought.
- I thought I did better than that.
- I know I tried my best.
- That's disappointing.
- Oh, *$#@, my parents are going to freak.
- My teachers must be so upset with me.
- I've let everyone down.
- I'm so stupid.
- What an idiot.

See how the first few statements are neutral? With statements like these, you're acknowledging your disappointment and surprise. You might even just tap through these phrases to neutralize them even more. Just tap the points and repeat the sentences.

The next statements reflect your stressed state when you get your report card. Notice how different these phrases feel. There's an urgency and an alarm associated with these statements. When you find yourself thinking thoughts like these—not just about report cards and grades—start tapping. Create a setup statement with the phrase that hits home with you. You might pick one and repeat that setup statement three times and do some simple reminder phrases. I want you to tap until you can get to more neutral thoughts.

Karate Chop: Even though I'm thinking, *Oh, *$#@, my parents are going to freak*, I love and accept myself.
Karate Chop: Even though I'm thinking my teacher must be so upset with me, I love and accept myself.
Karate Chop: Even though I'm thinking I've let everyone down, I love and accept myself.
Karate Chop: Even though I'm thinking, *I'm so stupid*, I love and accept myself.
Karate Chop: Even though I'm thinking, *What an idiot*, I love and accept myself.

Eyebrow: My parents are going to freak . . .
Side of Eye: I'm going to be grounded for life . . .
Under Eye: I'm going to be in such trouble . . .
Under Nose: My father is going to yell at me . . .
Chin: Or give me the silent treatment . . .
Collarbone: I'm so stupid . . .
Under Arm: What an idiot . . .
Top of Head: I'd rather be kinder to myself.

I recognize that you might have harsh consequences if you don't do well. I'm not suggesting that we will change the consequences with tapping, but we can take the sting out of them. Thinking negative thoughts about what happened and what might happen just adds to your stress. Tap yourself into neutral.

There's More to Explore

If you want to do some more tapping on school-related stuff, head over to page 208 and go deeper into this issue.

TAPFIRMATION

I'm always doing the best I can.

Chapter 12

TAPPING ABOUT BULLYING

No matter what you call it (bullying, being picked on, teasing) or what form it comes in (physical, emotional, verbal, cyber), being singled out in a hurtful way can have devastating effects. And it doesn't just happen at school. I want to help you reduce the sting of the bully's words, actions, and intentions. By tapping on how you're thinking and feeling about being picked on and reducing the pain of it, you might come to feel that you have a bit more power.

Many girls who experience bullying keep it to themselves, feeling embarrassed and even ashamed that they're being targeted. If you're experiencing bullying, I encourage you to tell someone: a parent, a caring adult, a teacher, a principal, a school counselor, or a friend. If it feels difficult to tell someone, here's some tapping to help you feel better about sharing.

Karate Chop: Even though I feel embarrassed that this is happening to me, I love and accept myself.
Karate Chop: Even though I feel stupid telling anyone, I'd rather have support around this.
Karate Chop: Even though I'm afraid to tell on the bully, I love and accept myself.

Eyebrow: I feel embarrassed . . .
Side of Eye: I'm feeling ashamed that I'm being picked on . . .
Under Eye: I'm afraid to rat on the bully . . .
Under Nose: So I'm trying to face it alone . . .

Chin: I'd rather have some support . . .
Collarbone: I deserve to have backup with this . . .
Under Arm: I don't have to face it alone . . .
Top of Head: Nobody should face this alone.

. . . .

CASSIDY'S COMMENT

I know this is a hard one to talk about, but it's an important one to tap about. Being bullied can seem like it's taking your light away, or taking away your power. You might be trying to be less shiny, and less you, but tapping will help you stay who you are. You may feel more comfortable at school and feel less intimidated by the bully. I know that won't happen for everyone, but the goal with tapping is for you to feel better and better within yourself. Please do this for yourself and tap on the stuff in this chapter. But also do the tapping exercises on everything in this book that applies to you, everything that bothers you. You will become stronger and stronger in general, and bullies just won't be interested in you.

. . . .

"I need help right now!"

Bullying leaves a mark, and I know that tapping can help erase that mark and help you move forward without carrying that heavy stress with you. I've created a bunch of setup statements for you here so you can jump right in and start tapping. One or more of these (or all of them!) may represent what you're dealing with right now. Please pick some (or all) of these setup statements, the ones that feel like the place where you need help, and create your own reminder phrases—just a couple of words is fine. I know there's a lot here for you to pick from; I wanted you to have lots of options so you can begin feeling a bit of relief as soon as possible.

Karate Chop: Even though it happened a long time ago and it's over, I still hurt and I love and accept myself.
Karate Chop: Even though this has been going on a long time, I still love and accept myself.

Karate Chop: Even though I am getting more and more tired of this, I love and accept myself.

Karate Chop: Even though it's exhausting to always have to protect myself, I'd rather feel safe.

Karate Chop: Even though I don't feel safe, I love and accept myself.

Karate Chop: Even though they're hurting my soul, I'm going to love and protect my soul.

Karate Chop: Even though what they do is so humiliating, I'm trying to love and accept myself.

Karate Chop: Even though they're messing with my mind, I focus attention on what I love about myself.

Karate Chop: Even though their words affect me, I love and accept myself.

Karate Chop: Even though they're saying things that aren't true, I love and accept myself and I know the truth.

Karate Chop: Even though I can't believe how cruel these kids are, I'm going to be kind to others.

Karate Chop: Even though it's shocking that they're getting away with being bullies, it's not fair and I'm going to be strong.

If you have a particular person who's been bullying you, chances are you're feeling like you have to protect yourself much of the time you're at school or anywhere this person might be. If just hearing their name or thinking of them makes your heart race, I suggest tapping through all the tapping points until you feel a little calmer when saying their name.

Remember we talked about the fight-or-flight or freeze thing we do when we're feeling under attack? When you're feeling unsafe on a daily basis, you're stuck in a pattern of being on high alert. I want to help you use tapping to calm the feeling of being on high alert while increasing your feeling of safety.

Also, remember we talked about the stress backpack you're carrying? I think that when you have a bully, you're carrying the weight and the energy of that person around with you in your backpack all the time. Let's empty your backpack and dump the bully.

Tap on the Specific Parts of Your Experience

A great way to deal with the bullying you've had is to tap on the specific parts of your bullying experience. It can help you take the pain out of the past experiences. Grab your notebook and write down some of the things the bully has done. Here are some possibilities to get you started. You'll see that I've put together the setup statements for you so you can start tapping.

- Name calling: Even though they're calling me names, I love and accept myself.

- Spreading gossip: Even though they're spreading gossip about me, I love and accept myself.

- Physical aggression: Even though they're physically picking on me, I love and accept myself.

- Being left out or ignored: Even though I'm suddenly being ignored, I love and accept myself.

- Ganging up: Even though they're ganging up on me, I love and accept myself.

- Getting teased: Even though I'm getting teased every day, I love and accept myself.

- Getting pranked: Even though they played that awful prank, I love and accept myself.

- Getting harassed on social media: Even though they keep posting things about me on social media, I love and respect myself.

It's not your fault!

Always remember that you deserve to be treated well. And nobody deserves bullying. No matter what, being bullied is not your fault. You are not weak, you've become a target for a bully. For now, they have some power and they likely have a team behind them. Tapping can help you feel powerful again and remember your own strength.

Karate Chop: Even though I think I'm weak, I'd rather feel strong.
Karate Chop: Even though I don't know what I've done to deserve this, I know it's not my fault.
Karate Chop: Even though that bully needs a whole team behind them, I should get a team.
Karate Chop: Even though they think I'm weak, I love and accept myself and my strength.

Karate Chop: Even though they have issues, I'm not the cause of their issues and I love and accept myself.

Karate Chop: Even though I don't know what to do about them, I'd rather remember how awesome I am.

Eyebrow: I think I'm weak . . .
Side of Eye: I'd rather feel strong . . .
Under Eye: But they need a whole team behind them . . .
Under Nose: I don't know what to do . . .
Chin: I'll remember how strong I am . . .
Collarbone: I am stronger than they are . . .
Under Arm: I'd rather be strong . . .
Top of Head: And remember my strength.

Get Your Power Back! Exercise

Often, girls who experience bullying don't feel like they have someone who's there to protect them. What we're going to do in this exercise is imagine that you have a personal protector. In your imagination, if you could be protected by someone, something, human or not, real or magical, who or what would it be? It could be a superhero you like, a powerful animal, an angel, a wizard, anything! Then I want you to think about and write down their characteristics: strong, powerful, kind, supportive, magical, protective—anything. Now create a picture in your mind. If you have the image in your mind, great. Draw it if you're an artist. If you want to find an actual image, do an online image search, using all the descriptive words you can think of. Save an image to your computer or phone and look at that image to help you feel like you have a protector. If you've chosen a superhero or an animal, you can probably find a toy version to carry around with you. However you picture your protector, do it every day and even several times a day. This really could help you feel more powerful.

When someone else is being bullied

We all know bullies and we have all witnessed people being bullied. I want you to notice what you think and feel when you witness someone being bullied. Think about the kid at school who always seems to be the target. I invite you to grab your notebook and write down some thoughts and feelings. I'll get you started:

When I think about that kid who gets bullied . . .
. . . I'm just glad it's not me.
. . . I feel powerless.
. . . I feel angry.
. . . I feel afraid.

Karate Chop: Even though I feel powerless, I'm glad it's not me and I love and accept myself.
Karate Chop: Even though I feel so angry at the bullies, I love and accept myself.
Karate Chop: Even though I'm afraid of them, I still love and accept myself.
Karate Chop: Even though their behavior is horrible, I'd rather be kind.
Karate Chop: Even though they're picking on people, I'd rather be kind.
Karate Chop: Even though they seem dangerous, I'd rather not be a bystander.
Karate Chop: Even though they're being cruel, I'll practice kindness.
Karate Chop: Even though it might not be cool, I'll be kind to those being bullied.

There's More to Explore

If you want to do some more tapping on stuff related to bullying and being treated badly, head over to page 214 and keep going deeper into this issue.

TAPFIRMATION
Their bullying is not my fault.

Chapter 13

TAPPING ABOUT PERFORMANCE

What kinds of things do you love to do? Does singing make your heart sing? Are you into playing a sport, an instrument, or a lead role in a dramatic production? Right now I want you to think about that thing you love doing. How do you feel when you think about picking up your guitar or kicking around a soccer ball? If you feel uplifted, full, and happy when you think about your favorite activity, I want you, right now, to do the Butterfly Hug (page 26). When you do that, you can tap in that feeling, and it's like downloading it into your whole body system. Think of it as your happy place. Then at another time, when you're feeling a little down or off your game, I want you to take a deep breath and remember how it feels when you think about doing what you love and do the Butterfly Hug again.

This is a great exercise for you to do as often as you want. If you're in the middle of doing homework and feeling stuck, just imagine that you're doing your thing—whether it's ballet, writing, or shooting baskets. If you're not actually doing the thing you love right now, just thinking about it will give you a boost because your brain doesn't really know the difference between doing something and thinking about doing that thing. So if you're feeling bummed, imagine just for a minute that you're doing the thing you love. A minute of daydreaming can boost your mood—but I don't recommend it while in class or while operating heavy machinery!

See how great it feels to deliberately think about the activity you love doing? Whether your area of performance is sport, music, dance, or slam poetry, there can be very rewarding times and there can be some challenging times. So what do you do when something interferes with feeling good about your performance? Whether you love writing but sometimes get writer's block, love shooting baskets but keep missing shots, or love performing but sometimes get stage fright, you're going to find out how to feel better and perform better.

Katherine loved playing piano, but almost quit!

Katherine was in ninth grade and loved playing piano. She felt joyful, happy, peaceful, and in the zone when she played and she had no problem practicing every day on top of going to her lessons. Katherine felt like she was learning a lot and improving as she practiced. When she practiced at home, she usually plugged headphones into her electronic keyboard and nobody could hear her play. But if she was home alone, she didn't wear her headphones. She loved hearing her music fill the room.

One day while home alone, she was working on a new, difficult piece. She was playing one part over and over and making lots of mistakes as she practiced, but she was determined to get it. She was focused and concentrating on her work and even though it was difficult, she was feeling great.

She didn't hear her father come in, so she was shocked when he yelled at her. "Katherine, would you stop making that awful noise? I can't believe we're spending all this money on lessons for you and this is how you sound! I hope you're not planning a music career, because at this rate that's never going to happen."

Katherine was torn out of her happy musical trance by her father's harsh words. She turned off her keyboard, went to her room, and lay on her bed. Her father's words felt devastating. He had basically said she was awful at piano, she was costing them money, and she had no hope of ever improving.

Has anything like this ever happened to you when you were learning and practicing, striving to get better at doing something you love? I know lots of people who, as teenage girls, quit their favorite activities altogether because they believed what those people said. But they didn't know tapping when they were in their teens. As adults, they regret losing their love of piano, dance, singing, sports, art, or whatever it was they gave up.

I don't want you to give up on something you love to do just because somebody said something insensitive and hurtful. If this has already happened to you, check out the tapping statements that Katherine used to come out of her state of shock and get back to doing what she loved. To adapt the statements to your situation, you can just write down what the critical person said to you and create your own wording from there. Check your level of intensity on a scale of 0 to 10 before you start tapping. You might be surprised at how much that criticism still hurts. Check again with your number after you've tapped through these or your own statements.

No matter what your beloved activity is, please tap along. We're not only tapping on what was said, but also on what Katherine was thinking and feeling about herself and music as a result.

Karate Chop: Even though I was in my zone and Dad broke in with his yelling at me, I love and accept myself.

Karate Chop: Even though he said my music was an awful noise, I love my music.

Karate Chop: Even though he complained about spending money on lessons for me, I still love and accept myself.

Karate Chop: Even though when I think about what he said, I feel shocked, I love and accept myself.

Karate Chop: Even though when I think about what he said, I feel humiliated, I love and accept myself anyway.

Karate Chop: Even though I now wonder if I'm really bad at piano, I'd rather remember that I love it.

Karate Chop: Even though he said I'd never make a career of piano, he only heard a few difficult seconds.

Karate Chop: Even though for a minute I considered quitting, I give myself permission to continue loving piano.

Karate Chop: Even though he judged my playing based on a few moments of a difficult piece, I love and accept myself.

Karate Chop: Even though he said those things, I am in charge of whether I believe him and I love and respect myself.

Karate Chop: Even though he said awful things, I know that I love music.

Karate Chop: Even though he almost interfered with my music, I love myself enough to keep practicing.

Eyebrow: He said awful things . . .
Side of Eye: I can't believe what he said . . .
Under Eye: Why would he say such awful things . . .
Under Nose: He's not usually so mean . . .
Chin: He said it was an awful noise . . .
Collarbone: But I was just practicing a part . . .
Under Arm: He shocked me out of my zone . . .
Top of Head: I was shocked . . .

Eyebrow:	First it was startling . . .
Side of Eye:	I thought I was alone . . .
Under Eye:	That was bad enough . . .
Under Nose:	But he was so mean . . .
Chin:	It's over now and I'm okay . . .
Collarbone:	I still love piano . . .
Under Arm:	I can still feel determined . . .
Top of Head:	To get better and better . . .

This is such a great story for you to tap along with because you can see how Katherine moved through these thoughts and feelings. Once she tapped on the shock of her father's surprise attack, Katherine realized that she was pretty upset about what her father said. She was angry with him for being so harsh and for making her consider quitting doing what she loved so much.

Katherine said, "I am so glad that I'd already learned tapping with my piano teacher because I really needed it that day. I was so shocked that my dad was so nasty that I considered making a giant, dramatic gesture and putting my keyboard in the trash can, making sure my father saw me do it. I was so upset that I was ready to quit forever. Then I got angry and tapped through that as well. That was it! I went back to my piano, put on headphones, and started practicing again."

But many people get frozen in the shock of the event. They get on the hamster wheel of doom and they keep replaying the bad moment and the bad feelings over and over. Don't do that! Tap instead. Tapping is antifreeze!

Here's more of Katherine's tapping that helped her shift from shocked to determined.

Eyebrow:	I'm so angry that he said that to me . . .
Side of Eye:	He totally shot me down . . .
Under Eye:	And tore me from my happy place . . .
Under Nose:	He was so nasty . . .
Chin:	I can take criticism . . .
Collarbone:	But that was mean . . .
Under Arm:	I'd rather let go of what he said . . .
Top of Head:	I'm sure he regrets it . . .

Eyebrow:	I'd rather resume loving piano . . .
Side of Eye:	It's mine . . .

Under Eye: I'm dumping his words from my hard drive . . .
Under Nose: I'm not letting them get in . . .
Chin: He said something in a moment . . .
Collarbone: That was devastating . . .
Under Arm: It's over and I'm ok . . .
Top of Head: I'm going to practice.

Katherine felt better, and she went back to her piano and put on headphones and started practicing again. A few times she noticed her frustration growing as she worked on the difficult part, so she stopped and did some tapping. Katherine told me, "I know I was still angry, so it was like I was spite-practicing. Like saying, 'I'll show you' to my dad. So no surprise that I couldn't get back in the zone and I kept getting stuck on that one part. I kept tapping."

Karate Chop: Even though I keep getting stuck on this part and it's too hard, I love and accept myself.
Karate Chop: Even though this part keeps messing me up, I love and accept myself.
Karate Chop: Even though my dad's interference messed me up, that's over now and I love and respect myself too much to keep thinking about it.
Karate Chop: Even though this bit is difficult, I'd rather be calm and coordinated.

Katherine said, "Then I took a deep breath. I was calmer! I played through it with fewer mistakes. It was so awesome, like my brain stopped reminding me that I was getting to the tricky part. And it stopped reminding me of that moment when my dad yelled at me. I am so glad that I started tapping immediately. It kind of freaked me out that I had a minute of thinking I'd quit, but I can see how people would just do that. Don't quit! Tap instead!"

Tapping to get over the bumps

You'll probably agree that practicing is necessary if you want to improve your skills and abilities. Adding tapping to your practice routine can help you be clear, focused, and present. But first, let's tap on any bumps you experience when you're practicing. What are your bumps when practicing? Maybe when you're singing your voice shakes when you're trying to reach a certain note, or you have trouble making a shot from a certain angle. Again, tap on all the statements even if they're about a different activity. I think I've covered a bunch here to get you started.

Karate Chop: Even though when I'm at the free-throw line I keep missing the shot, I love and accept myself anyway.
Karate Chop: Even though I get stuck on that line in my speech, I release that block now and I love and accept myself.
Karate Chop: Even though I can't make my fingers bend that way to reach the chord, I'd rather be loose.
Karate Chop: Even though I keep forgetting my lines, I'd rather have glue in my brain that my lines stick to.
Karate Chop: Even though I messed up a couple of times, and I keep expecting to mess up, I'd rather give myself a break and keep going.
Karate Chop: Even though I can't seem to crack my time in this race, I'm open to releasing my stress about it.
Karate Chop: Even though I feel stuck here, I'd rather picture myself there.

Keep tapping with your own reminder phrases as you go through the tapping points.

CASSIDY'S COMMENT

I use tapping all the time for sports, singing, acting, or whatever nerve-wracking activity I get involved in. If I'm nervous, it calms me, if I get stuck, tapping unblocks me. Trust me, if you want to get better at the stuff you love to do, add tapping.

Recovering from a disappointing performance

If you've ever had a rough performance (and most people have)—forgot a line in your school play, missed an "easy" basket in your game, or flubbed your piano recital—that kind of upset can get stored in your stress backpack, affect your future performances, and keep you from improving your skills. So when you think about your next show or game, sometimes your brain can remind you of that misstep and spark a worry: *What if that happens again?*

If you think you've stored a negative story about a past performance in your stress backpack, take some time to tap on what happened. Check your level of intensity and see how upset you are right now. Tapping can help alleviate the upset so you don't carry it with you to your next performance. And the more you get to practice your skills, the more you'll improve. Here are some example setup statements to get you started. You can plug in the facts of your own flub into the setup statement.

Karate Chop: Even though I froze onstage and forgot my lines, I love and accept myself.

Karate Chop: Even though I'm worried that I'll do that again, I want to remember that I'm in charge.

Karate Chop: Even though I made that mistake, I realize that I'm not perfect and I love and accept myself.

Eyebrow: I forgot my lines . . .
Side of Eye: I was so embarrassed to freeze onstage . . .
Under Eye: I can't believe I did that . . .
Under Nose: What if I do that again . . .
Chin: What if I do that every time from now on . . .
Collarbone: I realize I'm not perfect . . .
Under Arm: I'd rather be calm and confident . . .
Top of Head: I'm in charge.

Karate Chop: Even though I can't believe I missed that shot, I'd rather let it go and move on.

Karate Chop: Even though I disappointed my team and I feel awful, I love and accept myself.

Karate Chop: Even though I keep going over it in my head, it happened and it's over and I love and accept myself.

Eyebrow: I can't believe I missed that shot . . .
Side of Eye: I disappointed my team . . .
Under Eye: I feel so awful about it . . .
Under Nose: I keep replaying it over and over . . .
Chin: And I'm worried about my next game . . .

Collarbone: It's time to move on . . .
Under Arm: I always do my best . . .
Top of Head: I'd rather be calm and confident.

If in the future you have a disappointing performance, make sure you tap on it as soon as possible and avoid storing it in your stress backpack.

A past "failure" doesn't mean future failure

Another thing that can interfere with your ability to improve your skills is feeling like you've failed at something that you really wanted to do. If you've practiced and practiced but still didn't make the team, or didn't get the lead in the school play, you can use tapping to dispel the disappointment and help you continue pursuing what you love. Don't let your thoughts of failure make you freeze.

Karate Chop: Even though I'm so upset that I didn't get chosen, I love and accept myself.
Karate Chop: Even though I feel like a failure, I'd rather keep pursuing my dream.
Karate Chop: Even though I did my best but that wasn't good enough, I'm going to keep improving.

Eyebrow: I was sure I'd get chosen . . .
Side of Eye: I'm so upset that I didn't . . .
Under Eye: And I feel like a failure . . .
Under Nose: That's such a harsh term to use . . .
Chin: I know I did my best . . .
Collarbone: But I can improve for next time . . .
Under Arm: I want there to be a next time . . .
Top of Head: Quitting is not an option.

Did anyone ever tell you that you couldn't do it?

Have you ever had anybody tell you that you couldn't accomplish or achieve something? One of the main reasons people get stuck on the way to accomplishing their dreams is because somewhere along the way, somebody told them they'd never be able to do it, like Katherine's dad saying she'd never become a professional musician.

Many girls hear that their dreams of being professional singers, dancers, athletes, or writers are impossible. For that matter, many girls also hear that becoming a doctor, physicist, engineer, astronaut, or dentist is an impossible dream.

That's what I heard from my father when I was in high school. I'd always thought of becoming a writer (spoiler alert—I wrote this book!). When I was in tenth grade, my English teacher suggested I take creative writing as an elective the next year. It felt amazing to have my writing ability recognized by my teacher, whom I respected.

Unfortunately I had to get my parents' permission to take the special class. My father said, "Well, that's a stupid idea. Do you think you're going to become a famous writer or something? Let me tell you right now that you'll never make a living as a writer, so you're better off learning how to type."

I was 15 years old at the time and I can promise you I wasn't thinking about becoming a famous writer or even making a living as a writer. I just wanted to write and talk about writing and learn more about something I loved doing. And even though I didn't take the class but took typing instead, I kept on writing and wrote even more than I had before (probably out of spite). I never told my parents I was writing and I hid my work away. But as I got older and was considering what I wanted to do as work, as a career, all I wanted to do was write and be a writer.

Still, every time I considered jobs, I remembered my father's statement, "You'll never make a living as a writer." It was like he was an evil wizard and he'd waved his wand and cursed me with that statement. When I thought about going to university and taking writing courses, I remembered my father's pronouncement, so I studied something else instead. And even though I kept writing secretly, it wasn't until I did tapping to release the "curse" of my father's statement that I was able to write for a living.

I know for a fact that if it weren't for tapping, I wouldn't have written a book about tapping! I'm so glad I can share this with you now so you can get rid of the curse of someone telling you that you can't achieve your dreams.

Even though it might be painful, I do want you to think about something someone said to you that caused you to think differently about yourself, your goals, and your dreams. Did a coach tell you that you were an awful player, or a music teacher tell you that you would never be a good singer? Maybe an older brother or sister teased you about your dancing and told you that you'd never be any good. It doesn't matter who said it, why they said it, or whether they even meant it. What happens is that we keep thinking about what they said, we doubt ourselves, and we end up believing what they said was the truth. They're the older person, after all. They should know whether we'll be able to accomplish something. Wrong.

I don't believe you would be infused with your dream if it wasn't possible for you to achieve it. When someone tells you to face reality and focus your attention on doing something worthwhile instead of dreaming the impossible dream, start tapping.

Karate Chop: Even though they said I'd never make it as a [singer, writer, dancer, painter, photographer, soccer player, wrestler], I love and accept myself.
Karate Chop: Even though they told me to stop trying, I love and respect myself too much to listen to their "advice."
Karate Chop: Even though they said it was impossible to achieve that, I still want to try and I love and accept myself.
Karate Chop: Even though it hurts that they don't believe in me, I continue to believe in myself.
Karate Chop: Even though they didn't fulfill their dream, it doesn't mean that I can't fulfill mine.
Karate Chop: Even though they infected me with their statement, I am releasing the poison of their words.
Karate Chop: Even though their statement is like a potion that kept me from believing in myself, I'm tapping in the antidote now!
Karate Chop: Even though they said that almost nobody gets to be successful at what I want to do, I still want to keep doing what I love.

Achieving Your Dreams Tip

The first step to achieving your dreams and your goals is to think helpful, positive thoughts. It's difficult to do so when you're thinking about the unhelpful, negative things that people have told you about achieving your dreams. Please spend as much time as you need to and tap on any negative thoughts you're thinking about reaching your goals. Whether those thoughts come from someone else, or from your own internal critic, keep tapping. Of course you need to practice, study, and learn in order to increase your skill level, no matter what your chosen activity or subject is.

Thinking helpful thoughts is the best way to improve your performance. Tapping is the best way to release unhelpful, negative thoughts and infuse yourself with positive, helpful thoughts. Whether you feel terrified of your knuckle-cracking piano teacher or your bully of a swim coach who thinks yelling obscenities will motivate you, tapping will help you feel calmer.

There's More to Explore

If you want to do some more tapping on topics related to performance, head over to page 217 and keep going deeper into this issue.

TAPFIRMATION

As I practice, I'm getting better and better at something I love doing.

part five

TAPPING ON YOUR RELATIONSHIPS

. . . .

CASSIDY'S COMMENT

Are you stressing about your social life? Do you have a bunch of friends on social media but still feel alone? Maybe you feel shy and have difficulty making friends, or you're struggling with friendships that have ended suddenly. If you're older, you may be thinking about dating and having a romantic relationship with a boy, or with a girl. It's not your imagination that relationships, whether they are friendships or romantic ones, can feel like an emotional roller coaster.

Tapping will help you deal with disappointments and heartbreak and even help you figure out how you really feel about the people in your life.

. . . .

Chapter 14

TAPPING ABOUT YOUR FRIENDSHIPS

Do you think it's important to have a thousand Facebook friends? Are you collecting people by the numbers or are you connecting with people with your heart? That's a good way to think of making friends—connecting rather than collecting. You might think it's important to appear to have a large collection of friends. You might think you will look more popular if you have a lot of virtual friends, but is that enough for you?

Sometimes friendships happen by default. You live next door to someone and have hung out your whole life. Or you grew up with your dad's best friend's daughter. You didn't really have a choice when your mom was setting up playdates for you with other kids. But as you get older, your parents aren't arranging playdates for you anymore, and you get to independently choose your friends and acquaintances. You get to decide what kind of person you want to be, and you also get to decide what kind of people you want to surround yourself with.

Are you connecting or collecting?

How do you choose, and whom do you choose to include in your inner circle? Sometimes you might wait until people choose you to be their friends, but would they have been on your list? It may be tempting to hang out with the cool girls, or the popular girls, but are those the main qualities you want to have in a friend? Remember that you have a choice about whom you spend your time with.

Get out your notebook and think about your closest friends, your favorite people, and think about the qualities they have that you like. What do you value most in other people? Why did you give your BFF that title? Make some notes. Quite simply, the goal is to choose friends who have more and more qualities that you like. I want you to think about the people who are around you most often. Do you feel good when you're with them, or do you feel bad when you're with them? Remember that the goal is always to feel good.

At the same time, think about your own best qualities. Very often we find that we like being around people who have a lot in common with us, whether it's interests or values we share.

Have a look at the list of positive qualities below. Then grab your notebook and write down the qualities *you* look for in a friend.

Positive friend qualities

Fun and funny	Supportive
Kind	Thoughtful
Trustworthy	Loyal (They've got your
Forgiving	back)
Generous with their time	Optimistic
and attention	Positive
Authentic/real/not phony	Good listener
Nonjudgmental	Dependable

Think about friends or family who have these qualities. Then write down how you feel when you're with your friend or family member who has these positive qualities. You might feel *safe*, *loved*, *happy*, *understood*, *positive*, and *optimistic*. I'm sure you see that feeling good with the people you have around you is important to your well-being and you deserve to feel good.

Next, think about the qualities you *don't* like in the people around you. Make a list of these not-so-positive qualities. Here are some words to get you started, but I'm sure you can come up with lots more.

Not-so-positive friend qualities

Mean	Judgmental
Unkind	Phony
Negative	Jealous
Pessimistic	Unsupportive
Gossipy	Envious

How do you feel when you're around people who have these qualities? I know this may be difficult to think about because some of your friends and family may actually have these qualities. But I think it's important to pay attention to how you feel when you're around them. Do you feel positive and optimistic when you're with a friend who's negative and pessimistic? If you're a kind person, what's it like to be with someone who's mean, gossipy, and judgmental? Are you able to tell your friends your good news and know they'll be happy for you, or do you hesitate because you know they'll be jealous and sarcastic?

Try this round of tapping to help you unravel whether you're getting the most from your friendships. If you've been collecting people instead of connecting with them, you may not be getting your friendship needs met.

Karate Chop: Even though I sometimes feel bad about myself when I'm around them, I want to love and accept myself.
Karate Chop: Even though I don't feel good when I'm around that person, I love and respect myself.
Karate Chop: Even though I realize they're cool but they're not kind, I deserve to feel good around my friends.
Karate Chop: Even though I sometimes think I can't afford to be picky, I deserve to be treated well.
Karate Chop: Even though they're my only friends, I can be open to people who are more compatible.

Eyebrow: I feel bad about myself when I'm with them . . .
Side of Eye: I respect myself too much to keep feeling bad . . .

Under Eye: I don't feel good around them . . .
Under Nose: I deserve to feel good . . .
Chin: I know they're "cool" . . .
Collarbone: And that helps me feel cool . . .
Under Arm: But I don't feel good with them . . .
Top of Head: I deserve to be treated well...

Eyebrow: Cool isn't everything . . .
Side of Eye: I'd rather feel good . . .
Under Eye: I deserve to feel safe with my friends . . .
Under Nose: I deserve to have loyal friends . . .
Chin: I deserve to have kind friends . . .
Collarbone: I deserve to be treated well . . .
Under Arm: I can afford to be picky . . .
Top of Head: I'm going to pick my friends with intention.

What does that mean—to pick friends with intention? It means you have certain criteria, certain characteristics, that you need in a friend and you deliberately choose people who have these characteristics. Would the first list you made, the list of positive friend qualities, be a good representation of the kind of people you'd like to hang around with? I'd like you to consider referring to that list when you're considering new friendships and when you're evaluating existing friendships. You deserve to have good friends and to feel good when you're with them.

"It's hard making friends"

Let's do some general tapping about making friends. For some girls it's easy to make friends, and for some girls it's more difficult. And underlying the whole subject of making friends is the need and desire to fit in. You want to fit in somewhere and yet still be an individual. You want to belong somewhere and still be yourself.

Karate Chop: Even though it's hard to make friends, I am likeable and I love and accept myself.
Karate Chop: Even though I worry that people won't like me, I love and accept myself and I want to decide if I like them.

Karate Chop: Even though sometimes I don't want to approach people, I'd rather feel more comfortable.

Eyebrow: It's hard to make friends . . .
Side of Eye: But I know I'm likeable . . .
Under Eye: I worry they won't like me . . .
Under Nose: But it's important that I like them as well . . .
Chin: I have a hard time approaching people . . .
Collarbone: And being the first to say hi . . .
Under Arm: I'd rather feel more comfortable . . .
Top of Head: As I pick my friends . . .

Karate Chop: Even though I want them to like me, but I don't even know if I like them, I love and accept myself.
Karate Chop: Even though I want to be friends because they're cool, I wonder if they'd be on my list.
Karate Chop: Even though I want them to like me, I love and respect myself too much to change who I am to please them.

Eyebrow: I want them to like me . . .
Side of Eye: And I need to like me too . . .
Under Eye: They're cool and I want them to like me . . .
Under Nose: But I don't know what they're like inside . . .
Chin: So I don't know if I like them . . .
Collarbone: I deserve to be with likeable people . . .
Under Arm: I deserve to be liked . . .
Top of Head: For who and how I am.

"I want to be liked for who I am"

We want to be liked—that's natural. Generally when we meet people and we have stuff in common—we like similar things and have similar interests—we like each other and become friends. But people have different likes and dislikes, and they won't always match. Have you ever felt as if you had to give up stuff you liked in order to be liked by another person? Or pretend to like something that a new friend liked so that he or she would like you? Are you willing to do something that goes against your beliefs and values in an attempt to have certain people like you?

I'd like you to grab your notebook and write down some of the things you like to do. What kinds of activities, interests, ideas, music do you enjoy? This is important because often we don't really take the time to figure out what matters to us. Take some time to do that now.

Next, on a scale of 0 to 10, with 10 being the most you could like something, please give each of the things on your list a number. If reading is your favorite thing to do, then give it a 10. If you like cycling but not as much as reading, maybe you'll give it a 7.

Now ask yourself: If you made a new friend who didn't like reading, who thought reading was dumb, and thought people who read were dumb, would you give up reading? Would you give up cycling if a friend hated cycling?

Be authentic. Most girls say they want to be liked for who they are. I know that you can tap on some of the challenges you might have being your authentic self and begin to accept yourself the way you are. When you love and accept yourself, you may find that others also accept you for who you are.

Karate Chop: Even though I want to be liked for who I am, I'm going to love and accept myself the way I am.
Karate Chop: Even though sometimes I think I'm not good enough the way I am, I'd rather love and accept myself the way I am.
Karate Chop: Even though I still don't know who I am, I'd rather love and accept myself the way I am right now.
Karate Chop: Even though I'm still figuring out who I am, I deserve to be treated well anyway so I'll love and accept myself.
Karate Chop: Even though I think I have to change for people to like me, I'd rather be easier on myself.
Karate Chop: Even though I don't know if people like me, I think I'm pretty cool.

Eyebrow: I want to be liked for being me . . .
Side of Eye: I'm going to like me for being me . . .
Under Eye: I want to appreciate myself first . . .
Under Nose: When I like me . . . .
Chin: I feel good . . .
Collarbone: I'm figuring out who I am . . .
Under Arm: I'm pretty awesome . . .
Top of Head: I am someone I'd hang out with . . .

Eyebrow: I deserve to have good friends . . .
Side of Eye: I'm figuring out who I want to be friends with . . .
Under Eye: I have the right to choose my friends . . .
Under Nose: I deserve to be treated well . . .
Chin: By like-minded friends . . .
Collarbone: I don't have to change me . . .
Under Arm: I want to be me . . .
Top of Head: I deserve to be me with my friends.

"I feel rejected"

Everyone feels rejection at some point in their lives. Whether we don't get picked for a team or someone we have a crush on doesn't feel the same way about us, rejection can feel devastating. You might feel like you'll never get over it, but I assure you that things will feel better.

Let's do some tapping on this feeling. Right now, if you're feeling rejected by someone, please write down your level of intensity. How upsetting is it on a scale of 0 to 10? Try tapping on your karate chop point while repeating each of these setup statements three times. Create your own reminder phrases and do full rounds of tapping until you're feeling more at ease. Check in with your level of intensity as you go along.

Karate Chop: Even though they rejected me, I love and accept myself anyway.
Karate Chop: Even though I feel rejected, I still love and accept myself.

As you tap on feeling rejected, please take notice of the kind of thoughts that come to mind. It's really important to tap on these side effects before they take root.

Event	Thought
Something happens	You have a thought
I experience rejection	I'm not good enough
	I'm not lovable
	I'll never try again
	I must be ugly
	I must be _____

Please don't jump to conclusions about having been rejected. Some girls jump to the conclusion that they're "not good enough" after being rejected. By making the connection between the event (you get rejected) and the thoughts you have about it (*I'm not good enough*), you can pinpoint any assumptions that you might be making and tap on those.

Karate Chop: Even though I think I'm not good enough, I love and respect myself.
Karate Chop: Even though they I think I must not be lovable, I do love and accept myself.
Karate Chop: Even though I think they rejected me because I'm _____, I love and respect myself.
Karate Chop: Even though I don't know why they rejected me and I'm assuming I'm not good enough, I love and respect myself too much to make stuff up.

Eyebrow: I think I'm not good enough . . .
Side of Eye: That doesn't feel good . . .
Under Eye: I'd rather feel neutral . . .
Under Nose: I think I'm unlovable . . .
Chin: But that doesn't feel good . . .
Collarbone: I know I'm lovable . . .
Under Arm: Maybe they think I'm ugly . . .
Top of Head: Or too much of something . . .

Eyebrow: Or not enough of something . . .
Side of Eye: I'd rather not make stuff up . . .
Under Eye: I may never know what happened . . .
Under Nose: But thinking awful things about myself feels awful . . .
Chin: The truth is we're not a match . . .
Collarbone: I'd rather be with people who match . . .
Under Arm: I know I was rejected . . .
Top of Head: But I love and respect myself.

There's More to Explore

I know relationships are complicated and there might be lots more to tap on around choosing, making, and keeping friends. I think you're doing really well creating setup statements and reminder phrases on your own, but I'm also happy to give you some more ideas. So if you want to do more tapping on subjects related to your friendships, head over to page 221 and keep going deeper into this issue with tapping.

> ## TAPFIRMATION
> *I know I deserve to be treated well.*

Chapter 15

TAPPING ABOUT YOUR ROMANTIC LIFE

This chapter is going to be like a magical travel guide to help you use tapping to navigate everything from crushes to heartbreak. Romantic relationships can be super complicated and they can get really messy and they can also be exciting and fun. Whether you're interested in boys or in girls, I have tapping tips to help you get through pretty much everything.

Even if you're not ready to date, or your parents won't let you date, you're probably curious about the world of love and romance, and that's normal and fun. It might be uncomfortable to have a conversation with adults about love and attraction, but I encourage you to do so if you have questions and curiosities. This chapter isn't a replacement for talking to an adult who might answer your questions about dating, romance, and sex, but it might help you get more comfortable with talking about it with a caring adult. I hope that by reading this chapter and doing the tapping exercises, you'll feel empowered in your current and future romantic relationships and that you'll understand the importance of being treated well and with respect.

Let's tap about crushes

Having a crush on someone can be exciting and confusing, scary and fun. You might talk to all your friends about your crush, or you might keep it to yourself. When you see the person you like, you might want to hide, or you might want to make eye contact.

When you have crushes, you're getting an idea of the kind of person you might want to have a romantic relationship with later on. You're learning about yourself as well. You're learning what you like about people and what you expect from your relationships. It is valuable in romantic relationships, as in friendships, to think about the qualities you want the person to have—and having crushes helps you figure out what those qualities are.

You might also notice that while your friends are having crushes on boys, you find yourself having a crush on a girl. That's normal and natural, and all the tapping phrases I have below are written for girls who have crushes on girls *and* for girls who have crushes on boys.

These setup statements are meant to help you feel more calm and confident about your crush. You're not tapping to reduce your crush or get over it, just to be more comfortable with it. Let's get started!

Karate Chop: Even though I like that person, what if they don't like me? But I love and accept myself no matter what.

Karate Chop: Even though I have this crush, I love and accept myself.

Karate Chop: Even though I feel crushed by this crush, I love and accept myself.

Karate Chop: Even though these feelings are confusing, I love and respect myself.

Karate Chop: Even though I keep waiting for a sign that they like me too, I love and accept myself.

Karate Chop: Even though I really want them to like me, I still love and accept myself.

Karate Chop: Even though I desperately want them to like me, I love and respect myself too much to be desperate.

Karate Chop: Even though this feels intense, I love and accept myself.

"What if I do have a crush on a girl?"

I assure you again that it's normal and natural to have a crush on someone of the same sex. It may feel confusing, on top of the other crush-related feelings you're having, and we'll do some tapping about that for you specifically. While your friends are talking about the boys they have crushes on, it might feel difficult for you to mention that your crush is a girl. You might feel left out of the talk and excitement of it all. It's important to share only what you feel comfortable sharing. Lots of girls keep their crushes secret, and it's important to remember that your feelings are personal and private and you're in charge of them.

Karate Chop: Even though my friends have crushes on boys and I think I have a crush on a girl, I love and accept myself no matter what.
Karate Chop: Even though on top of having a crush, it's a crush on a girl, I still love and accept myself.
Karate Chop: Even though I feel left out of my friends' conversations because I don't want to talk about my crush, that's okay, I still love and accept myself.
Karate Chop: Even though I have this crush, I want to be true to myself and my feelings.
Karate Chop: Even though it's confusing—of course it's confusing—I love and respect myself.
Karate Chop: Even though I have these feelings, I want to honor my feelings and love and accept myself no matter what.
Karate Chop: Even though I feel stressed about my feelings, I love and accept myself no matter what.
Karate Chop: Even though I feel butterflies around her, I love and respect myself.
Karate Chop: Even though I have these feelings, I don't have to put a label on them and I love and accept myself.
Karate Chop: Even though I have these feelings, I accept my feelings and myself.

Remember you don't have to label your feelings—just enjoy them. Your friends who are crushing on boys are enjoying it: the drama, the daydreaming. You deserve to be excited and fluttery about your crush too. Enjoy having a crush!

If you feel worry, or you're thinking unhelpful thoughts about what it might mean to have a crush on a girl, I will get you started on tapping about those thoughts and feelings.

Karate Chop: Even though I might have a crush on a girl and I wonder if I'm gay, I love and accept myself.
Karate Chop: Even though I wonder if I'm gay, I might be and I might not be. Either way, I love and accept myself.
Karate Chop: Even though I think I might be gay, I love and accept myself.
Karate Chop: Even though I'm worried that people will talk about me, I love and respect myself.

Karate Chop: Even though I'm worried about disappointing my family if I'm gay, I love and respect myself.

Karate Chop: Even though I don't want to be different from other girls this way, I love and respect myself.

Karate Chop: Even though it's complex, right now I don't have to label myself, and I love and accept myself.

Let's tap about romantic relationships

You know there are many different forms of stress that a romantic relationship might bring up. You're already super solid about tapping, so make sure you're tapping to calm your nerves and soothe your hurts, worries, and concerns as you think about dating someone. Remember that even good, exciting, fun, butterflies-in-stomach stress is still stress that adds to the stress you're already feeling. If you're feeling overwhelmed, tap. If you're agonizing over sending a message, calling, or texting, tap.

Here, I want to give you some tapping solutions to help you with some common stuff that comes up for girls who are exploring romantic relationships. I'm not giving you advice, but I am reminding you of the stuff we've tapped about regarding friendships and the kind of people you want to be around. I want you to be able to be yourself and feel good around your friends, and especially around someone you're dating. I want you to remember, above all, that you deserve to be treated well.

"I like someone but they don't like me that way"

It's the worst feeling, and I'm pretty sure that most girls have liked someone who didn't feel the same way about them. You may want to write down some of the things that made you like the person (the way we did earlier, in Chapter 14) to help you keep track of the qualities you like in people. But that may not help with the hurt. So let's tap.

Karate Chop: Even though I like them but they don't like me, I still love and accept myself.

Karate Chop: Even though I don't know why they don't like me that way, I still like me.

Karate Chop: Even though I really hoped they would like me, maybe friendship is an option, and I love and accept myself no matter what.

Karate Chop: Even though I'm hurt that they don't like me, I know I'll be okay.
Karate Chop: Even though I really wanted to be their girlfriend, I'd rather choose someone who also chooses me.
Karate Chop: Even though I'm upset, I deserve to be treated well.

Eyebrow: I really liked them . . .
Side of Eye: But they don't feel the same . . .
Under Eye: They don't like me that way . . .
Under Nose: It hurts . . .
Chin: But I'm still awesome . . .
Collarbone: I feel rejected . . .
Under Arm: But I'm still likeable . . .
Top of Head: I'm still lovable . . .

Eyebrow: I'd rather choose someone who chooses me . . .
Side of Eye: Unrequited love hurts . . .
Under Eye: But I'm okay . . .
Under Nose: If I thought they were awesome . . .
Chin: The next person I like . . .
Collarbone: Will be amazing . . .
Under Arm: I deserve to be treated well . . .
Top of Head: I am still awesome.

"Someone likes me and I don't like them that way"

If you don't like someone in a romantic way but they want to have that kind of relationship with you, how do you say no to them? How would you want someone to say no to you? My guess is that you'd want them to be kind, and you would want them to keep it between you, meaning you wouldn't want them to blab to the whole school that you liked them and they rejected you.

That being said, it's also so important to know that you're in charge. If you don't like someone in a romantic way, that's great! You're getting an idea of the kinds of people you want to have relationships with and the kinds of people you don't. You are certainly never expected to like everyone who likes you! You're in charge here and you don't owe any explanations for why you're not interested. Seriously. Be kind, be firm, and don't apologize. You have no reason to apologize because you're doing nothing wrong when you don't have romantic feelings for someone. Saying no to someone in this way allows them to move on and consider other people.

If it's a girl who expresses having feelings for you, it's the same as if it's a boy. But also remember that she may be feeling these feelings for the first time, she's as scared and nervous as you can imagine, and she is really going out on a limb to bring this up with you. She may never have told anyone that she might have romantic feelings for girls, so it's especially important to honor her privacy. She's trusted you with this private information about herself. Again, don't apologize, just be kind and be firm.

I know that some girls might agree to date someone because they don't want to hurt that person's feelings or to seem unkind. The truth is we never want to hurt someone else and we might end up feeling bad about letting someone down. Please tap on these sorts of feelings as well. You definitely should not go out with someone because he or she wants you to or you feel like you should.

No matter who's professed their interest in a relationship with you, I want you to do this tapping about having to reject someone else.

> **Karate Chop:** Even though they want a relationship with me, I don't feel the same and I love and respect myself.
> **Karate Chop:** Even though I have to say no to them, I am going to be kind.
> **Karate Chop:** Even though they think I should say yes to them, I'm in charge and I'm saying no.
> **Karate Chop:** Even though I feel bad for rejecting them, I know I'm doing it kindly.
> **Karate Chop:** Even though I'm saying no, I appreciate their asking, and I love and respect myself too much to try to please them.
> **Karate Chop:** Even though I feel bad, I'm not doing anything I need to apologize for by saying no, and I love and accept myself.

Please go ahead and tap through all the tapping points while repeating your reminder phrases.

"I'm not ready . . ."

Whatever it is that you're not ready for, remember you're in charge! Whether it's dating in the first place, kissing someone, or more, you are in charge. If your friends are telling stories of their relationships and you're feeling left out, remember that you're in charge of whether or not you're ready. Whether you're interested in girls or boys, you're in charge and you're the only one who gets to say when you're ready.

Karate Chop: Even though I'm not ready, I love and respect myself.
Karate Chop: Even though my friends are giving me grief because I'm not ready, I remember I'm in charge.
Karate Chop: Even though I like my person but I'm not ready to go further, I love and respect myself.
Karate Chop: Even though they might be pressuring me to go further, I'm not ready and I'm in charge.
Karate Chop: Even though they want more than I'm ready for, I'm in charge!
Karate Chop: Even though my friends are bugging me, I'm going to stay true to myself.
Karate Chop: Even though I'm curious, I don't think I'm ready and I'm in charge.

Red flags

You know how you sometimes have a feeling, a little warning voice telling you to pay attention to whether or not you're being treated well? I want you to be aware of these little red warning flags and pay attention to them. I don't mean that I want you to be on high alert waiting for your person to start acting like a jerk, but I want you to take note if you have a weird inkling that something is not right. If something doesn't feel right, take a note, write it in your journal, or talk to someone about it.

So if you've been hanging out with a new person and enjoying each other's company and seemingly out of nowhere, they say something harsh or unkind, take note of it. How do you feel when they talk to you this way? Is it okay for someone to speak to you this way? What if it happens again? Remember you're in charge. You can do some tapping to help you figure out what to do if you have some red flags raising in your relationships.

Karate Chop: Even though things were going well and then they said that mean thing, I love and respect myself.
Karate Chop: Even though it surprised me that they said that, I'm paying attention and I love and accept myself.

THE TAPPING SOLUTION FOR TEENAGE GIRLS

Karate Chop: Even though I thought they were so kind, and that was an unkind remark, I love and respect myself.

Karate Chop: Even though it's not okay to talk to me that way, I remember that I'm in charge.

Karate Chop: Even though that was unkind, I deserve better and I love and respect myself.

The dreaded breakup

Whether you initiate it or the other person does, a breakup hurts. My first breakup was unexplained and came out of nowhere. I was dating a boy at the end of the school year and we hung out for a couple of months, and then he went away with his family on vacation and simply didn't phone again when he got back. I waited by the phone (this was back in the day when phones were attached to the house) for a few days. No phone call. I thought maybe their vacation had been extended, so I got a girlfriend to go to the baseball field at the time I knew his team would be practicing, to see if he was there. He was. I was devastated.

But not only was I devastated, I was confused, upset, and angry, and my self-confidence took a hit. I automatically thought I'd done something wrong, I wasn't good enough, and so on. And I sat in my room for a few days and brooded about that. Unfortunately tapping hadn't been invented yet. So I'm going to take you through all the tapping I would have done when I was 16 and had my first heartbreak.

Karate Chop: Even though they broke my heart, I love and accept myself.

Karate Chop: Even though they didn't call me when they said they would, I love and accept myself.

Karate Chop: Even though all of a sudden it was over, I still love and accept myself.

Karate Chop: Even though I can't believe they didn't bother telling me we'd broken up, I love and accept myself.

Karate Chop: Even though I was truly hurt, I'm okay now.

Karate Chop: Even though I thought there must be something wrong with me, clearly there's something wrong with them.

Karate Chop: Even though I feel devastated, I'll be okay, and I love and accept myself.

Karate Chop: Even though what they did was ignorant, I still love and accept myself.

Karate Chop: Even though I thought they were perfect for me, clearly there will be someone better for me.
Karate Chop: Even though I'm so confused, I'd rather not blame myself and feel even worse.
Karate Chop: Even though I think I did something wrong, what was wrong was what they did.
Karate Chop: Even though I'm imagining all kinds of negative things, I'd rather imagine feeling peaceful.

I'm going to share with you a thought that I had after a couple of days in my room worrying about what happened with that boyfriend. It's like I was hit by lightning, and I don't know where the idea came from, but I have never forgotten it. I think of it all the time when I'm facing disappointment.

If I thought this was so great, then just
imagine how great my next relationship will be!

And just like that, I was over the heartbreak. I'm actually grateful for the experience because in the midst of it, I found this phrase, which helped guide me through inevitable disappointments in my future. I've used this phrase to feel better about jobs I didn't get and friendships and other relationships that ended. I've shared it with friends and with many clients who are facing disappointment.

And guess what? Many years later, at a high school reunion, that same boy apologized to me.

When you have to do the breaking up

Yes, it's difficult! Just remember that you deserve to be treated well and if that isn't happening, it might be time to break up. There are as many reasons for breakups as there are humans. Maybe you're simply not feeling "it" anymore. Whatever the reason, you have to be true to yourself and how you're feeling, and what (and who) is right for you. This might be a difficult conversation to have, so here are a bunch of setup statements to help you shake off your nerves and get your confidence rolling.

Karate Chop: Even though I have to end my relationship, I love and accept myself.
Karate Chop: Even though I feel bad that I have to break up with them, I still love and accept myself.

Karate Chop: Even though it's hard to break up, I love and respect myself too much to stay when I'm not happy.

Karate Chop: Even though I don't want to hurt them, I also don't want to hurt myself by staying.

Karate Chop: Even though they did something that's not okay, I still love and accept myself.

Karate Chop: Even though I learned a lot in this relationship, I now know more of what I want in a relationship.

Eyebrow: I need to break up with them . . .
Side of Eye: I'm just not feeling it anymore . . .
Under Eye: And that's okay . . .
Under Nose: I know they're a good person . . .
Chin: I feel bad . . .
Collarbone: But I have to do what's right for me . . .
Under Arm: I don't want to hurt them . . .
Top of Head: But I don't want to hurt me either.

Eyebrow: If I thought they were great . . .
Side of Eye: And they were great . . .
Under Eye: Imagine how great . . .
Under Nose: My next person will be for me . . .
Chin: I'd rather take care of myself . . .
Collarbone: And end the relationship . . .
Under Arm: With kindness . . .
Top of Head: I'm doing this for me.

There are so many amazing things that can happen in relationships, and I want you to be able to enjoy yourself in all your relationships with the people you choose to have in your life. Please return to this chapter regularly because as you change and grow, what you need from your relationships will change too. Tapping will help you make good decisions about people in your life, and when the inevitable hurts come along, tapping will help you heal.

There's More to Explore

I think we've covered a lot about romantic relationships, crushes, and more. But there's even more here for you to explore. Just turn to page 229.

TAPFIRMATION

I choose to have awesome people in my life.

Chapter 16

TAPPING ABOUT SEX

As a teenage girl, you're probably becoming curious (or you already know you're curious!) about the topic of sex. When you were younger and first learning about sex, you might have thought it was something super gross. As you've gotten older, you might find that you're interested, nervous, scared, excited, or uncomfortable with your thoughts and feelings about sex. As your body changes and your hormones change, thinking about sex is normal, and so is having sexual feelings. I'm not teaching sex ed here; I just want you to feel comfortable in your body while you're experiencing this very normal hormonal change that your body's undergoing.

. . . .

CASSIDY'S COMMENT

Ugh, stuff about sex is so uncomfortable, and for lots of girls it's almost impossible to talk about! It's supposed to be this totally normal part of life, but there's so much attached to it that it becomes this uncomfortable, forbidden topic. Some girls are lucky and they can talk to their parents about sex the same way they talk about anything important. Other girls feel like they have to sneak information or try to talk with their friends. This chapter will be great for you because this isn't a sex ed book but you get to tap about your thoughts and feelings and curiosities about sex and to know how normal you are to have this curiosity.

. . . .

Let's do some super-simple tapping about this complex topic!

Karate Chop: Even though I'm curious about sexual topics, I love and accept myself.
Karate Chop: Even though I'm curious and looking for things to read about sexuality, I love and accept myself.
Karate Chop: Even though I'm curious about what sex is all about, it's normal to be curious and I love and accept myself.

Eyebrow: I'm curious about sexual topics . . .
Side of Eye: It's normal to be curious . . .
Under Eye: I'm not perverted . . . I'm curious . . .
Under Nose: I want to learn more . . .
Chin: That's normal . . .
Collarbone: My body feels different . . .
Under Arm: That's normal . . .
Top of Head: I'm curious and that's normal.

Eyebrow: My friends talk about it a lot . . .
Side of Eye: It all sounds so weird . . .
Under Eye: It's normal to be curious . . .
Under Nose: I wonder what it's all about . . .
Chin: I'm just learning about it . . .
Collarbone: I'm in charge of my body . . .
Under Arm: I'm normal and curious . . .
Top of Head: I'm in charge of my body . . .

It can be hard to talk about sex stuff

Your hormones change as you mature, and your reproductive hormones are responsible for sexual feelings you might be having. You might want to talk to someone about these feelings but find it difficult to do so. Tapping can help with that.

Karate Chop: Even though I have these feelings I want to talk about but I'm uncomfortable, I'm normal and I accept myself.
Karate Chop: Even though I'm nervous talking about this, I'd rather be comfortable talking about this normal thing.

Karate Chop: Even though I want to ask lots of questions but I'm uncomfortable, I still love and accept myself.

Eyebrow: I'm curious . . .
Side of Eye: My body is changing . . .
Under Eye: I'm having physical feelings . . .
Under Nose: I want to talk about it . . .
Chin: But I'm not comfortable . . .
Collarbone: My parents are not comfortable . . .
Under Arm: If it's so normal . . .
Top of Head: Why are people so weird about it . . .

Eyebrow: I'm nervous . . .
Side of Eye: I'd rather be comfortable . . .
Under Eye: And ask the questions . . .
Under Nose: That I need answers for . . .
Chin: This is important to me . . .
Collarbone: I'm not weird for wondering . . .
Under Arm: I'm curious . . .
Top of Head: I'm curious about my body.

CASSIDY'S COMMENT

Talking about sex with parents can be awkward for everyone. So here's a trick! If you want to have a sex talk with your parents, then get them tapping about their own discomfort talking to you about it. Give your mom this chapter and get her to tap for herself. Or when you're having a conversation that's difficult, both of you do the Butterfly Hug tapping (page 26). That way you get to have a conversation and hopefully both of you will be a little calmer and less agitated about it.

"I'm having feelings for a girl"

As I mentioned in the last chapter, it's absolutely normal for a girl to have romantic or sexual feelings for girls. It's just a fact. Lots of people around the world have different opinions, beliefs, and ideas about that fact. But the fact is, it's normal. It might be confusing, but it's normal. So if you think you might have feelings for a girl, you're normal. If you think you might have feelings for a boy as well—guess what? Normal.

Even so, your teenage years can feel tumultuous, and if on top of typical tumult you feel like you might have romantic or sexual feelings for a girl, that may feel confusing. If this is happening to you, here's some tapping for you to try.

Karate Chop: Even though I might have feelings for a girl, I love and accept myself.
Karate Chop: Even though my friends are always talking about boys, and I like a girl, I love and accept myself.
Karate Chop: Even though romantic feelings are confusing, I accept that I have these feelings.
Karate Chop: Even though right now I'm not sure, I love and respect myself no matter what.
Karate Chop: Even though it's supposed to be normal to feel this way, I give myself permission to accept myself.
Karate Chop: Even though lots of people have different opinions about being gay, I love and respect myself.
Karate Chop: Even though I might be having these feelings, the fact is, I'm normal and I love and respect myself.

Please tap along with these phrases as much as you need to. And check out Chapter 15, where there's a whole section for girls who might have crushes on girls. It's normal and I want you to feel more and more comfortable being who you are.

If you're thinking about having sex

Now that's a big decision—like, a major life decision. The biggest thing to remember is: *Your body—your decision*. And when you weigh all the information you have about sex, tapping can help you make the right decision for you.

Karate Chop: Even though I'm thinking about having sex, I think I'll learn more about it first.

Karate Chop: Even though lots of people have different opinions about sex, I love and respect myself.

Karate Chop: Even though some people think I should and some say I shouldn't, I still love and accept myself.

Karate Chop: Even though I'm feeling some pressure in my relationship, it's my body and my decision.

Karate Chop: Even though I'm curious, I love and respect myself too much to make a hasty decision.

It is a big decision and you might think it's the right decision . . . and then you might change your mind. You have the absolute right to change your mind and say no. Anytime!

There's More to Explore

You're doing an awesome job tapping about this complex topic. If you'd like to do more tapping about the topic of sex, then scoot over to page 232.

TAPFIRMATION

That happened, it's over, and right now I'm okay.

THERE'S MORE
TO EXPLORE

. . . .

It's great that you're still reading! Because there's a lot more to explore. I had so many ideas for things you might want to tap on that I wanted to give you as much as the space in this book would allow. You'll see that this part of the book matches up with the chapters you've just read, and the issues you can tap about here will relate to the issues we talked about in the chapters.

If you've just opened to this part of the book, welcome! If you don't know about this tapping thing yet, I suggest hopping over to Chapter 2 to learn the technique. Then you can easily use it on any of the issues in the book.

. . . .

From Chapter 4: There's More to Explore about Your Body and Your Appearance

Be kind to your body

In Chapter 4 we talked about being more comfortable with and kinder to your body. Here are some more tapping phrases you can use if you find you're being harsh about a certain body part.

Karate Chop: Even though I don't like my butt, I love and accept myself.
Karate Chop: Even though I hate my nose, I love and accept myself.
Karate Chop: Even though I wish my boobs were different, I'd rather love and accept myself and my boobs.

Eyebrow: I don't like my _____
Side of Eye: I hate my _____
Under Eye: I keep telling parts of my body . . .
Under Nose: That they're not good enough . . .
Chin: I'm being mean to my body . . .
Collarbone: I'd rather be kinder to my body . . .
Under Arm: I don't want to listen to people . . .
Top of Head: Saying mean things to me . . .

Eyebrow: But I keep saying mean things . . .
Side of Eye: To my boobs . . .
Under Eye: Mean things to my butt . . .
Under Nose: I'd like to apologize to my body parts . . .
Chin: For being mean to you . . .
Collarbone: I'd like to love and accept . . .
Under Arm: All parts of me . . .
Top of Head: I accept all parts of me.

Your body is changing

It's just a fact that your body's changing and that can feel uncomfortable. It might even feel painful as your bones actually grow. It can be weird to notice that almost overnight you have bigger breasts, you're taller, and you don't look like yourself any-more. You might notice that you're getting curves where there weren't curves before. The best thing you can do for yourself is tap through all these changes, pay attention to how you're feeling about new "developments," and tap with the goal of staying connected to your body and staying friends with your body.

> **Karate Chop:** Even though my body is changing, I love and accept myself and my new body.
> **Karate Chop:** Even though my body is changing and it's super weird, I love and accept myself.
> **Karate Chop:** Even though I feel uncomfortable in my body, I love and accept myself and my changing body.
> **Karate Chop:** Even though I cover myself up sometimes, I'd rather love and accept myself.

> Eyebrow: My body is changing . . .
> Side of Eye: I know it's normal . . .
> Under Eye: But I'm pretty uncomfortable . . .
> Under Nose: It seems like it's changing pretty fast . . .
> Chin: I sometimes cover myself up . . .
> Collarbone: My brain doesn't know what to do with these changes . . .
> Under Arm: But this is my body . . .
> Top of Head: I'd rather feel at peace with my body.

How do you feel? Even if I'm not reminding you to do so, make sure you check your level of intensity and notice how you're feeling after tapping. If you still feel some intensity, do another round or two of tapping. Because your body is changing, you might want to do this tapping exercise a few times a month and throughout your teenage years as you continue to grow and change.

"I'm feeling fat and I'd rather feel thinner"

Lots of media messages are bombarding girls about being thin. You see web articles dedicated to shaming celebrities who've gained weight, and articles celebrating how someone fit herself into size-0 clothes. I'm not going to show you any tapping about losing weight! Instead, you can tap on the feelings you're having about your weight, whatever those feelings are.

Karate Chop: Even though those images make me feel bad about myself, I'd rather feel more neutral.

Karate Chop: Even though my friends are always talking about being fat, I'd rather love and accept myself now.

Karate Chop: Even though when I think I look fat I feel awful, I'd rather love and accept myself more often.

Karate Chop: Even though I sometimes call myself fat, I love and respect myself too much to keep talking to myself that way.

Eyebrow:	Looking at those images . . .
Side of Eye:	Makes me feel bad about myself . . .
Under Eye:	I think I look fat by comparison . . .
Under Nose:	My friends are always talking about fat . . .
Chin:	It feels awful focusing on fat . . .
Collarbone:	I'd rather focus on my awesomeness . . .
Under Arm:	I love and respect myself too much . . .
Top of Head:	To keep talking to myself that way . . .

Eyebrow:	Instead of focusing on fat . . .
Side of Eye:	And feeling bad about myself . . .
Under Eye:	And looking at impossible images . . .
Under Nose:	I'd rather be okay with how I look right now . . .
Chin:	I'd rather have more confidence about my body . . .
Collarbone:	I'd rather stop comparing myself . . .
Under Arm:	To impossible, airbrushed standards . . .
Top of Head:	I'd rather be easier on myself.

From Chapter 5: There's More to Explore about That Time of the Month

"Suddenly my period started!"

If your worst nightmare is unexpectedly getting your period in the middle of a pool party, you're not alone! Many girls experience an irregular cycle and can't count on their monthly visitor showing up every 28 days on the nose. If you've had an unwelcome surprise in the past, don't let that stop you from living your life and having adventures. Here's some tapping that can help you feel better about the embarrassment.

Karate Chop: Even though my surprise period had me seeing red, I love and accept myself.
Karate Chop: Even though I was so embarrassed that my period suddenly started, I love and accept myself.
Karate Chop: Even though everyone in class knew I'd started my period, I love and accept myself.
Karate Chop: Even though I wasn't ready for this, I love and accept myself.

Eyebrow: Suddenly it was there . . .
Side of Eye: I'm so embarrassed . . .
Under Eye: Everybody knows . . .
Under Nose: I wasn't ready for this . . .
Chin: Why is something so normal . . .
Collarbone: So shameful and embarrassing . . .
Under Arm: I can't believe everyone saw the stain . . .
Top of Head: I'd rather feel comfortable.

How you feel about your skin

Having troubled skin is stressful enough without adding your troubled feelings about it. I hope this tapping will help to alleviate some of the emotional distress associated with having skin problems.

Karate Chop: Even though I have acne, I love and accept myself.
Karate Chop: Even though I want to avoid everything when my skin's like this, I'd rather feel calm.
Karate Chop: Even though I get anxious when my skin's like this, I love and accept myself anyway.
Karate Chop: Even though I feel kind of ashamed, I love and accept myself.
Karate Chop: Even though I feel so ugly right now, I love and accept myself.

Karate Chop: Even though my life is a disaster because of my acne, I love and accept myself.

Karate Chop: Even though I can't look anyone in the eye because of my skin, I love and accept myself anyway.

Eyebrow:	I have acne . . .
Side of Eye:	I want to avoid everything . . .
Under Eye:	I feel ashamed . . .
Under Nose:	It's wrecking my life . . .
Chin:	I get so anxious . . .
Collarbone:	I can't look at anyone . . .
Under Arm:	I feel so ugly . . .
Top of Head:	I'd rather feel neutral . . .

Eyebrow:	My skin is a mess . . .
Side of Eye:	I feel so anxious . . .
Under Eye:	I feel so ugly right now . . .
Under Nose:	I want to avoid everyone . . .
Chin:	I can't look at anyone . . .
Collarbone:	I'm hating my skin right now . . .
Under Arm:	I'm so frustrated . . .
Top of Head:	I've tried everything . . .

Eyebrow:	I don't know what to do about it . . .
Side of Eye:	I get so upset . . .
Under Eye:	I'd rather feel calmer . . .
Under Nose:	I'd like to release this skin stress . . .
Chin:	I don't feel like myself . . .
Collarbone:	I feel so ashamed . . .
Under Arm:	I'd rather be kinder to myself . . .
Top of Head:	And kinder to my face.

From Chapter 6: There's More to Explore about Your Emotional Health

Tapping about feeling guilty

Feeling guilty is a normal response when you've done something that you regret because it hurt someone or was wrong or illegal.

Karate Chop: Even though I feel guilty because I lied to my friend, I love and accept myself.

Karate Chop: Even though I went out with a new friend and lied about it, I'll try to love and accept myself.

Karate Chop: Even though I feel guilty because it would hurt my old friend's feelings, I love and accept myself.

Karate Chop: Even though I want to have more friends, I forgive myself.

Eyebrow: I feel so guilty . . .
Side of Eye: She'd be hurt if she knew . . .
Under Eye: But I want more friends . . .
Under Nose: And I feel bad . . .
Chin: I lied to my friend . . .
Collarbone: I didn't want to hurt her . . .
Under Arm: I wonder if I should tell her anyway . . .
Top of Head: I'd like to feel better about this.

"I worry about making decisions"

For some people, it's difficult to make decisions. They can't decide between strawberry and vanilla ice cream, what to study at school, what to wear to school, and so on. If you think you have trouble making decisions in general, or maybe you have a big decision approaching and you get tied up in knots thinking about how you're going to choose between A and B, do some tapping right now.

To start, get your notebook and write down the level of intensity you feel about decision making. Notice if it seems general or if you have discomfort about a specific decision you are expected to make right now. If there are specific things you have to decide upon, write them down in your notebook. I'm sure this tapping will help:

Karate Chop: Even though I worry that I will make the wrong decision, I love and accept myself.

Karate Chop: Even though I don't know how to make this decision, I love and accept myself.

Karate Chop: Even though neither choice feels like the right choice, I wonder if there's a third choice.

Karate Chop: Even though I don't know whether A or B is the right choice, I'm open to noticing how each feels.

Karate Chop: Even though making this decision is stressful and I feel it in my stomach [or head, heart, hands], I love and accept myself.

Eyebrow: I don't know what choice to make . . .
Side of Eye: Neither one feels right . . .
Under Eye: There's no clear yes or no . . .
Under Nose: I'm so stressed about this decision . . .
Chin: What if I make the wrong choice . . .
Collarbone: Like last time . . .
Under Arm: I regret that decision . . .
Top of Head: So I don't trust myself to make the right choice.

"I regret making that decision"

Most people have made a choice at some point in their lives that they wish they hadn't made. Keep tapping on this next part.

Karate Chop: Even though after I made that choice I instantly regretted it, I love and accept myself.

Karate Chop: Even though I chose A instead of B and have been beating myself up about it ever since, I love and accept myself.

Karate Chop: Even though I wish I'd made a different choice, it's behind me and I'd like to move on.

Eyebrow: I really blew it that time . . .
Side of Eye: I wish I'd chosen differently . . .
Under Eye: I should have listened to my gut . . .

186

Under Nose: Instead I listened to my friend . . .
Chin: I've been beating myself up about it . . .
Collarbone: I'd like to give myself a break . . .
Under Arm: It happened and it's over . . .
Top of Head: I want to trust myself again.

Karate Chop: Even though I made that decision, I did my best with the information I had and I love and accept myself.
Karate Chop: Even though I chose wrong, I'm okay now.
Karate Chop: Even though I made a wrong choice, it doesn't mean I'll always make the wrong choice.

Eyebrow: I made that mistake once . . .
Side of Eye: It doesn't mean I'm doomed to make bad choices . . .
Under Eye: I forgive myself for making that choice . . .
Under Nose: It's time to move on . . .
Chin: And practice trusting myself again . . .
Collarbone: I did my best with the information I had . . .
Under Arm: I wonder if A or B is right for me now . . .
Top of Head: I'm opening to hearing my inner voice.

From Chapter 7: There's More to Explore about Your Parents' Relationship

In Chapter 7 you read about Kayla and how she used tapping to help her deal with, in her words, the "messed-up stuff that was happening with my parents." Here are some more of the things that Kayla and I tapped on together around her parents' problems and eventually their separation and divorce. She wanted me to share them with you, knowing they'd help you as well.

The announcement

It's a shock to hear that your parents are separating or divorcing. What's your level of intensity right now when you think of them announcing their separation? Please start tapping:

Karate Chop: Even though it was a shock to hear they were divorcing, I love and accept myself and I'm okay.
Karate Chop: Even though I'm still in shock, I love and accept myself and I'm okay.
Karate Chop: Even though I don't know what it means, I love and accept myself.

Eyebrow: I'm in shock about this news . . .
Side of Eye: It was a shock to hear this . . .
Under Eye: I'm in shock . . .
Under Nose: I acknowledge that I'm in shock . . .
Chin: I don't know what it means . . .
Collarbone: I can't believe it . . .
Under Arm: Right now, I'm okay . . .
Top of Head: I'm going to be okay.

Check in with this feeling of shock, check your level of intensity, and tap on these phrases until you're feeling less shocked. Sometimes it can feel like you froze in that moment and went numb, and so here are some more reminder phrases you may want to use:

Eyebrow: I think I froze when they told me . . .
Side of Eye: I'm numb right now . . .
Under Eye: I don't know what to think . . .
Under Nose: I don't know what to do . . .
Chin: Feeling numb is normal . . .
Collarbone: I don't have to figure anything out right now . . .
Under Arm: I'd rather feel calmer . . .
Top of Head: But I know I'm freaking out . . .

Eyebrow: I can't believe this is happening . . .
Side of Eye: I kind of saw it coming . . .
Under Eye: But I didn't know what to do . . .
Under Nose: And I don't know what to do now
Chin: I acknowledge my feelings . . .
Collarbone: Of course I have feelings about this . . .
Under Arm: They say it's not about me . . .
Top of Head: But I'm part of this family . . .

Eyebrow: Is it my fault?
Side of Eye: They say it's not my fault . . .
Under Eye: I'm going to choose to believe them . . .
Under Nose: It is not my fault . . .
Chin: It is their marriage and divorce . . .
Collarbone: And it affects me . . .
Under Arm: But it is not my fault . . .
Top of Head: It's not my fault.

Karate Chop: Even though my parent is leaving and I think it's my fault, I love and accept myself.
Karate Chop: Even though I feel a mixture of guilt and sadness, I love and accept myself.
Karate Chop: Even though they say it's not my fault, I think I'll believe them.
Karate Chop: Even though I know they're leaving my other parent and I think they're leaving me too, I'd rather feel calmer.
Karate Chop: Even though I'm feeling desperate right now, I'd rather feel calmer.

Eyebrow: My parent is leaving . . .
Side of Eye: I think it's my fault . . .
Under Eye: I think it's about me . . .
Under Nose: I feel so sad . . .
Chin: And I feel so guilty . . .
Collarbone: I must have done something . . .
Under Arm: I think it's my fault . . .
Top of Head: But they said it's about them, not me . . .

Eyebrow: I want to believe that it's not my fault . . .
Side of Eye: I'm going to believe that it's not my fault . . .
Under Eye: The sadness is enough to deal with . . .
Under Nose: I don't want to add guilt to the mix . . .
Chin: The sadness is enough . . .
Collarbone: It's normal to feel sad . . .
Under Arm: I don't know if I'll feel happy again . . .
Top of Head: But it's okay to feel happy again . . .

Eyebrow:	I know their marriage is ending . . .
Side of Eye:	And my parent is leaving . . .
Under Eye:	They're leaving me too . . .
Under Nose:	I feel desperate . . .
Chin:	But I want to remember . . .
Collarbone:	Right now, I'm okay . . .
Under Arm:	I'm going to be okay . . .
Top of Head:	I am not at fault.

If your parents are divorcing, please bookmark this section, return to it again and again, and tap daily while going through this. It's important to remember that it's okay to be happy, to be a teenage girl, and to do the things you love to do even if there is upset in your household.

"What's going to happen to me [or to us kids]?"

This can be a frustrating time too, because your parents might not have all the answers about what happens next for you or for themselves, especially if this is a sudden and shocking split. The chart below helps you separate your thoughts and feelings and untangle some of the overwhelming sensations that go along with thinking and feeling a jumble of things all at once. Tapping can help you feel less freaked out and hopefully more calm while the next steps unfold.

Thought	Feeling
You have a thought	That creates a feeling
What's going to happen to me?	I feel afraid
No, it's not going to be okay	I'm feeling pessimistic
Everything is upside down	I feel resentful
Am I going to have to move?	I feel insecure
I can't believe they bailed	I'm so angry at them for doing this

Karate Chop: Even though I don't know what's going to happen to me, I love and accept myself.

Karate Chop: Even though I feel afraid, I love and accept myself.

Karate Chop: Even though I can't stop thinking about this, I love and accept myself.

Eyebrow:	What will happen to me . . .
Side of Eye:	I'm afraid right now . . .
Under Eye:	I know they're really upset . . .
Under Nose:	But I'm upset too . . .
Chin:	And I'm afraid . . .
Collarbone:	Because I don't know what will happen to me . . .
Under Arm:	I don't have any control here . . .
Top of Head:	I can't stop thinking about it all.

Karate Chop: Even though they say everything will be okay and I don't see how it can, I love and accept myself.

Karate Chop: Even though I'm feeling pessimistic, I acknowledge how I'm feeling and I love and accept myself.

Karate Chop: Even though I don't know if or when things are going to be okay, I'd rather feel calmer now.

Eyebrow:	They say things will be okay . . .
Side of Eye:	How do they know . . .
Under Eye:	I can't see how things will ever be okay again . . .
Under Nose:	That's how I feel right now . . .
Chin:	I'm feeling pessimistic right now . . .
Collarbone:	That's how I'm feeling right now . . .
Under Arm:	I'd rather feel calmer . . .
Top of Head:	I'd rather feel more relaxed.

Here are some phrases that really helped Kayla when she didn't know what was next for her and her family.

Karate Chop: Even though everything is upside down and I'm feeling resentful, I love and accept myself.

Karate Chop: Even though I don't even know where I'm going to live, right now I'm okay.

Karate Chop: Even though I feel guilty for thinking about myself, I love and accept myself.

Karate Chop: Even though I can't believe they bailed on their marriage, I love and accept myself.

Karate Chop: Even though I can't believe this is happening, right now I'm okay.

Eyebrow: Everything is upside down . . .
Side of Eye: I feel resentful . . .
Under Eye: Where am I going to live . . .
Under Nose: I feel selfish for worrying about myself . . .
Chin: I feel guilty thinking about myself . . .
Collarbone: But these are my thoughts and feelings . . .
Under Arm: And I acknowledge my thoughts and feelings . . .
Top of Head: This is how I'm feeling . . .

Eyebrow: It's normal to have questions and concerns . . .
Side of Eye: They might not have answers . . .
Under Eye: But I still have questions . . .
Under Nose: It's my life too . . .
Chin: I can't believe they bailed on each other . . .
Collarbone: And bailed on me too . . .
Under Arm: I'd rather feel calmer . . .
Top of Head: I'd rather feel more peaceful . . .

Eyebrow: I'd rather feel more peaceful . . .
Side of Eye: I'd rather feel calmer . . .
Under Eye: What if everything works out . . .
Under Nose: What if I'm okay . . .
Chin: This is a big change in my life . . .
Collarbone: I'm curious about what will happen . . .
Under Arm: And while it's happening . . .
Top of Head: I'm going to be in charge of how I'm feeling.

"My parent has a new person—gross!"

What happens when your parent brings a new relationship into their life and therefore into your life? You might be super happy that your parent has met someone, you might have mixed feelings about it, and you might be upset about it. And you might feel all these feelings at once. That's a lot, right?

Event	Thought	Feeling
Something happens	You have a thought	That creates a feeling
Dad has a new girlfriend	What about Mom?	I feel uneasy about this
	Mom will feel bad	I feel worried
	What if I hate his new person?	I feel guarded, insecure
	That was fast	I feel confused
And I'm not supposed to tell Mom	It's not my secret	I feel uncomfortable
	I just want everyone to be happy	I feel nervous

Karate Chop: Even though my dad has a new person and I feel uneasy, right now I'm okay.
Karate Chop: Even though I'm not supposed to tell Mom and I feel uncomfortable, I love and accept myself.
Karate Chop: Even though that was fast, I love and accept myself.
Karate Chop: Even though I feel worried about this new person, I'd rather feel more neutral right now.
Karate Chop: Even though I know Mom will feel bad, it's not my job to protect her, and I love and accept myself.
Karate Chop: Even though I'm afraid I will hate this new person, I'd rather be curious about them right now.

Eyebrow: There's a new person . . .
Side of Eye: What about Mom . . .
Under Eye: I feel so worried right now . . .

Under Nose: Mom will be so upset . . .
Chin: That was fast . . .
Collarbone: I feel guarded right now . . .
Under Arm: I'm feeling insecure about this change . . .
Top of Head: Right now everything's okay . . .

Eyebrow: I'm feeling confused . . .
Side of Eye: And I feel uneasy about this . . .
Under Eye: It's more stress . . .
Under Nose: After a stressful time with the divorce . . .
Chin: This is too much right now . . .
Collarbone: I'd rather feel peaceful . . .
Under Arm: I'd rather feel calmer . . .
Top of Head: Right now everything is okay.

"They want me to keep it secret"

Sometimes parents may ask you to keep quiet about something that they don't want your other parent to know about. Maybe they don't want your other parent to be hurt, but whatever the reason, it's super uncomfortable for you. You can tap on your discomfort.

Karate Chop: Even though I'm supposed to keep this a secret and I feel uncomfortable, I love and accept myself.
Karate Chop: Even though this isn't my secret to keep, I love and accept myself.
Karate Chop: Even though I just want everyone to be happy, I'm choosing happiness for myself and I love and accept myself.
Karate Chop: Even though I'm nervous about this secret, I'd rather be calm and I love and accept myself.
Karate Chop: Even though I feel bad knowing this information, it's not my job to take care of everyone and I love and accept myself.

Eyebrow: I'm uncomfortable with this secret . . .
Side of Eye: This isn't my secret . . .
Under Eye: It is too much to ask . . .
Under Nose: I'm not in charge of protecting them . . .

Chin: I'm in charge of me . . .
Collarbone: It's not right that they asked me to keep the secret . . .
Under Arm: I just want everyone to be happy . . .
Top of Head: I pick happiness for myself.

Please tap on whatever thoughts and feelings arise as you consider this issue. It may feel like your thoughts are bouncing around everywhere. Tap as they bounce. The bouncing is an indicator that you're unsettled about this. Keep tapping and eventually there will be just one or two things that feel troubling.

"I don't like my parent's new person"

I'm not trying to make you like the new person. But it's important that you have a way to address and tap on whatever feelings you do have about him or her. You may be pulled between how you think you should feel, how your parent wants you to feel, and how you actually feel. Let's tap to sort this out.

Karate Chop: Even though I don't like this new person, I love and accept myself.
Karate Chop: Even though my parent is upset because I don't like this person, I still love and accept myself.
Karate Chop: Even though I don't like this person, I'd rather feel more neutral, and I love and accept myself.
Karate Chop: Even though I feel guilty about my other parent if I'm nice to this new person, I love and accept myself.
Karate Chop: Even though I think I have to express my disapproval about this new person and it's stressful, I love and accept myself.
Karate Chop: Even though it's hard to like the new person because I feel like I'm not supposed to like them, I love and accept myself anyway.
Karate Chop: Even though this is a lot to deal with, I'd rather enjoy being a teenage girl!

Doesn't it feel good to tap and get all those thoughts off that hamster wheel of doom? Go back and tap as many times as you need to—and that might be anytime your parent talks about their new person. Tapping to feel neutral is for you and your peace of mind.

Finding out stuff about a parent

Remember we said earlier that a separation might be sudden and you might not get to know the details? Sometimes you do start to hear details and they can be upsetting to learn about. So if you've found out something about your parent that's upsetting, here's some tapping for you.

Karate Chop: Even though I found out this thing about my parent, I love and accept myself.
Karate Chop: Even though I thought I knew my parent, and this feels unsettling, I love and accept myself.
Karate Chop: Even though I didn't know my parent would do something like that, I love and accept myself.

Eyebrow: I found out something about my parent . . .
Side of Eye: It's unsettling to know this about them . . .
Under Eye: I thought I knew them . . .
Under Nose: I can't believe they did that . . .
Chin: It's nothing to do with me . . .
Collarbone: But I feel super weird about this . . .
Under Arm: What does this mean . . .
Top of Head: I'd rather be more neutral about this information . . .

Eyebrow: Even though they did this . . .
Side of Eye: They're still my parent . . .
Under Eye: And they still love me the same way . . .
Under Nose: I'm hurt and upset . . .
Chin: I'd rather feel calmer about this . . .
Collarbone: I don't understand it now . . .
Under Arm: And I don't have to . . .
Top of Head: I'd rather feel calmer.

Adding a stepfamily

You can have a ton of thoughts and feelings about a change in living situations with a new person and their kids entering the picture and potentially your home. I'm going to say it again—this is a lot to take in!

Karate Chop: Even though I don't like sharing my parent with stepkids, I love and accept myself.

Karate Chop: Even though these new kids are in my life, I'm confident in my relationship with my parent.

Karate Chop: Even though I don't know these people and I'm supposed to live with them, I love and accept myself.

Karate Chop: Even though on top of everything else, there are these new people and I feel overwhelmed, I'd rather be calmer.

Karate Chop: Even though I'm afraid my parent will like the stepkids better, I love and accept myself.

Karate Chop: Even though I don't feel like I can be myself around them, I love and accept myself.

From Chapter 8: There's More to Explore about Your Relationships with Parents and Family

"They don't listen to me"

"You never listen to me!" Have you ever said that to your parent, sibling, teacher, coach? Sometimes you don't feel like they understand what you're saying, and sometimes they're distracted by work, the Internet, phone, or whatever, and they're just not paying attention to you.

Karate Chop: Even though when they're not listening to me I think they don't care about me, I love and accept myself anyway.

Karate Chop: Even though I feel frustrated when they don't listen to me, I love and accept myself.

Karate Chop: Even though my parent is so distracted all the time, I love and accept myself.

Karate Chop: Even though they don't seem to care what I'm saying, I love and accept myself.

Karate Chop: Even though they're too busy to hear what I'm saying, I love and accept myself.

Eyebrow: They never listen to me . . .
Side of Eye: I feel like they don't care . . .

Under Eye: They don't want to know me . . .
Under Nose: They don't care about me . . .
Chin: They don't care about what's important to me . . .
Collarbone: They're so distracted all the time . . .
Under Arm: They're so busy all the time . . .
Top of Head: I feel invisible . . .

Eyebrow: I am important . . .
Side of Eye: What I have to say is important . . .
Under Eye: Even if they know better . . .
Under Nose: I want to be heard . . .
Chin: I am important . . .
Collarbone: I am visible . . .
Under Arm: I love and respect myself . . .
Top of Head: Even when they don't listen.

Pressure to be the best at everything

Maybe your parents, coaches, or siblings are super competitive and you're feeling like the pressure to be the best is getting stressful. This tapping will be helpful whether you're feeling pressure academically or in sports or creative performance.

Karate Chop: Even though they're never satisfied with what I achieve, I love and accept myself.

Karate Chop: Even though they want me to beat everyone, I'd rather just do my best.

Karate Chop: Even though they want me to be *the* best, I'd rather just do my best.

Karate Chop: Even though my parents are very competitive, I'd rather keep doing my best.

Karate Chop: Even though the pressure takes the fun out of sports, I enjoy doing my best.

Karate Chop: Even though I feel so much pressure, I love and accept myself.

Karate Chop: Even though if I don't win, I'm afraid they won't love me, I love and accept myself.

Karate Chop: Even though I'm so afraid to disappoint them, I love and accept myself.

Eyebrow: They're never satisfied . . .
Side of Eye: They're so competitive . . .
Under Eye: I'd rather be happy with my achievements . . .
Under Nose: I'm actually doing well at school . . .
Chin: I'm afraid they will be disappointed . . .
Collarbone: I'm afraid they won't love me . . .
Under Arm: I feel so much pressure . . .
Top of Head: It's getting to be too much . . .

Eyebrow: They just want me to win . . .
Side of Eye: They don't care if I'm happy . . .
Under Eye: I don't enjoy doing these activities . . .
Under Nose: There's so much pressure . . .
Chin: I love and respect myself . . .
Collarbone: I'd love to love that activity . . .
Under Arm: I release the pressure from myself . . .
Top of Head: I just want to enjoy myself.

From Chapter 9: There's More to Explore about Your Siblings and Conflicts

"My parents favor my sibling"

Sometimes you may have the sense that your parents favor a sibling over you. It may seem like your older sister gets more advantages and that may seem unfair. Your younger brother may get more attention and have more done for him by your parents. It may not actually be the case that your parents favor your sibling, but when it feels like that's the case, that feels awful.

Karate Chop: Even though they treat my sister like she's so special, I love and accept myself.
Karate Chop: Even though they like my brother more than me, I love and accept myself.
Karate Chop: Even though my sister can do no wrong and I get blamed for everything, I love and accept myself.

Eyebrow: She gets special treatment . . .
Side of Eye: And I get treated like crap . . .
Under Eye: They like my brother better . . .
Under Nose: They love her more than me . . .
Chin: She can do no wrong . . .
Collarbone: I get blamed for everything . . .
Under Arm: It's so unfair . . .
Top of Head: They get away with everything.

Stuff isn't fair

We know that when things seem unfair to you, it might also feel like your sibling is being favored over you. So let's explore how thinking something is unfair feels for you. How often do you think that something at home is unfair toward you? Let's make a list of things that feel unfair in your world. I'll get you started, and please grab your notebook and write down your own.

- Older sister gets to stay out later.

- Younger sister doesn't have to do chores.

- It's unfair that they treat me like a kid.

- It's not fair that I'm just categorized as a terrible teen.

- It's not fair that I can't have a smartphone.

How does it feel when things seem unfair? That's an important part of your setup statement.

I think this is unfair	I feel
Older sister gets to stay out later	Irritated
Younger sister doesn't have to do chores	Frustrated
It's unfair that they treat me like a kid	Discouraged
It's not fair that I'm just categorized as a terrible teen	Angry
It's not fair that I can't have a smartphone	Jealous

Karate Chop: Even though it's unfair that she gets to stay out later and I feel irritated, I love and accept myself anyway.

Karate Chop: Even though it's unfair that my little sister doesn't have to do chores and I feel so frustrated, I love and accept myself.

Karate Chop: Even though it's unfair that they keep treating me like a kid and I feel discouraged, I'd rather feel neutral.

Karate Chop: Even though it's unfair that I'm labeled a terrible teen, and I feel angry about that, I know I'm not terrible.

Karate Chop: Even though it's unfair that I can't have a smartphone, and I'm jealous of my friends who do, I love and accept myself.

Eyebrow: It's unfair . . .
Side of Eye: Life is unfair . . .
Under Eye: She gets to stay out later . . .
Under Nose: I have to do chores . . .
Chin: My little sister has no responsibility . . .
Collarbone: It's unfair . . .
Under Arm: I feel irritated . . .
Top of Head: I feel frustrated . . .

Eyebrow: When I get called a terrible teen . . .
Side of Eye: I feel so angry . . .
Under Eye: It's not fair to label all teenagers that way . . .
Under Nose: It's unfair that I can't have a new phone . . .
Chin: I feel so jealous . . .
Collarbone: It's so unfair . . .
Under Arm: I'd rather feel neutral . . .
Top of Head: I want to feel neutral.

From Chapter 10: There's More to Explore about Your Schoolwork

More about test anxiety

When you're about to take an exam or test, how do you feel just before and during? Here are some examples.

- My brain hurts.
- I get sweaty all over.
- My heart races just thinking about the test.
- I get butterflies in my stomach.
- I feel like barfing.
- I'm so nervous.

What are you thinking before an exam? Are you thinking positive or neutral thoughts or is your mind struggling with negative, unhelpful thoughts? Here are some examples of unhelpful thoughts:

- What if I run out of time?
- I never do well in this class.
- I can't think straight.
- I can't organize my thoughts.
- What if I forget everything?

Take any or all of these that apply to you and create your tapping statements. Tap yourself into helpful, positive thinking before your exams or tests.

Procrastination

While it just means that you're putting something off that you have to do, procrastination can be complex. First do some general tapping on procrastination and see what you notice. Then we'll move on to tapping on some specific reasons you might be procrastinating.

Karate Chop: Even though I'm procrastinating, I love and accept myself.

Karate Chop: Even though I know I'm procrastinating, I'd rather get things done now.

Karate Chop: Even though I'm putting this off, I'm also putting off the feeling of accomplishment and I love and accept myself.

Karate Chop: Even though procrastinating today makes tomorrow more stressful, I'd rather get it done today.

Karate Chop: Even though I'm putting it off but I need to do it, I'm in charge of doing my homework.

Karate Chop: Even though I'm tempted to procrastinate but I don't want it to become a habit, I'd rather do my work.

Eyebrow: I know I need to do my homework . . .
Side of Eye: I know I need to study . . .
Under Eye: I'm putting it off . . .
Under Nose: But I'd rather get it done . . .
Chin: I'm putting off doing it . . .
Collarbone: But also putting off celebrating finishing . . .
Under Arm: I'm in charge and I'm going to do it . . .
Top of Head: I'd rather celebrate finishing . . .

Eyebrow: I'm tempted to put it off . . .
Side of Eye: But I know it's stressful when I do that . . .
Under Eye: Putting it off today . . .
Under Nose: Makes tomorrow stressful . . .
Chin: I'd rather get it done . . .
Collarbone: I'd rather be in charge of getting it done . . .
Under Arm: I'd rather avoid making procrastination a habit . . .
Top of Head: And enjoy the accomplishment.

Are you rebelling?

Are you putting off math homework because you don't like your math teacher? Are you procrastinating on your studying because your parents keep reminding you to study? You might not even know if that's the problem. Just tap anyway because the goal is to help you feel better and reduce your stress about the work you have to do.

Karate Chop: Even though they keep nagging me to study and I don't want to give in, I love and accept myself.

Karate Chop: Even though they think I should be studying all the time and I don't want to study at all, I'd rather find a happy place in the middle.

Karate Chop: Even though they're bugging me to study, I'd rather decide to study for myself.

Karate Chop: Even though I might be rebelling, I am in charge of whether I do study and do my homework.

Karate Chop: Even though I'm rebelling by procrastinating, I'm the one who faces the consequences if I don't get it done.

Eyebrow: I might be rebelling by procrastinating . . .
Side of Eye: I keep putting off things . . .
Under Eye: That they keep telling me to do . . .
Under Nose: Rebelling is stressful . . .
Chin: If I keep procrastinating . . .
Collarbone: I'm the one with consequences . . .
Under Arm: But they keep nagging . . .
Top of Head: They keep bugging me . . .

Eyebrow: Maybe I think that if I do study . . .
Side of Eye: Then they'll win . . .
Under Eye: I'd rather do my work for me . . .
Under Nose: I know I have to get this done . . .
Chin: It's a requirement of my course . . .
Collarbone: I'm open to the possibility . . .
Under Arm: That I can release the rebellion . . .
Top of Head: And do the work.

Karate Chop: Even though I can't stand my math teacher so I put off doing math, I love and accept myself.

Karate Chop: Even though I can't do math without thinking about the teacher, so I put it off, I'd rather be more neutral.

Karate Chop: Even though I don't want to give respect to my teacher by doing homework, I respect myself.

Eyebrow: I do not like that teacher . . .
Side of Eye: I don't respect them . . .
Under Eye: And doing their homework shows respect . . .
Under Nose: So I put off doing the homework . . .
Chin: I keep thinking of the teacher . . .
Collarbone: As I do the homework . . .
Under Arm: I'd rather focus my attention on myself . . .
Top of Head: And on what I want to achieve.

Feeling stuck

Feeling stuck is so frustrating, and it leads to getting distracted, procrastinating, and avoidance. Consider whether it's time to ask for help, or set aside the problem you're stuck on and work on something else. Always, try tapping.

Karate Chop: Even though I am stuck on this problem so I'm putting off dealing with it, I love and accept myself.
Karate Chop: Even though I'm stuck right now, I am open to movement forward.
Karate Chop: Even though I feel stuck in this subject, I wonder if I can ask for help.

Eyebrow: I was doing so well . . .
Side of Eye: Now I feel stuck . . .
Under Eye: Stuck feels scary . . .
Under Nose: I'd rather move ahead with this . . .
Chin: Stuck is temporary . . .
Collarbone: I release the fear of being stuck . . .
Under Arm: I'd rather feel like this is easy . . .
Top of Head: I'm open to feeling like this is effortless.

"I'm just lazy"

Lazy is such an awful word, I think. If someone says you're being lazy, it can feel very upsetting and you can feel like it discounts the hard work you're doing.

Karate Chop: Even though my parents keep saying I'm lazy, I love and accept myself anyway.

Karate Chop: Even though when I don't jump to do what they ask, they say I'm lazy, I'd rather feel energized.
Karate Chop: Even though I've been labeled lazy, so why bother doing stuff, I love and accept myself.

Eyebrow: They've given me a label . . .
Side of Eye: That I don't like . . .
Under Eye: But I can't fight it . . .
Under Nose: They've always said I'm lazy . . .
Chin: They must be right . . .
Collarbone: They're my parents . . .
Under Arm: But what if they're wrong . . .
Top of Head: I'd rather feel energized . . .

Eyebrow: Just because they've labeled me lazy . . .
Side of Eye: It doesn't mean that I am lazy . . .
Under Eye: Procrastinating is a habit . . .
Under Nose: I want a new energized habit . . .
Chin: It's okay to prove my parents wrong . . .
Collarbone: I'm going to do this for me . . .
Under Arm: I reject that lazy label . . .
Top of Head: And do my best for me.

Tap while doing your homework

Karate Chop: Even though I feel so frustrated that I'm not getting this homework, I love and accept myself.
Karate Chop: Even though I feel confused when I'm trying to learn something, I'd rather feel calm and comfortable.
Karate Chop: Even though I get overwhelmed when I don't understand something, I'd rather feel neutral.
Karate Chop: Even though I can't read this properly, I'd rather feel neutral.
Karate Chop: Even though I feel angry when I can't understand something, I love and accept myself.

Eyebrow:	I get overwhelmed . . .
Side of Eye:	It's hard for me to learn this stuff . . .
Under Eye:	I get so frustrated . . .
Under Nose:	I'd rather feel calmer . . .
Chin:	I'd like to feel more neutral . . .
Collarbone:	And less frustrated . . .
Under Arm:	I'd rather have peace about learning . . .
Top of Head:	Even if something feels difficult.

School is stressful. Period!

As I said earlier, based on the survey by the American Psychological Association, 83 percent of teenagers say that school is a big source of stress in their lives! Whether it's the academic part of school that stresses you out, or dealing with the social aspects of being around hordes of people, the bottom line is that it's stressful. Here's a super simple setup statement with a mash-up of reminder phrases.

Karate Chop: Even though school is stressful, I love and accept myself.
Karate Chop: Even though school is stressful, I love and accept myself.
Karate Chop: Even though school is stressful, I love and accept myself.

Eyebrow:	School is stressful . . .
Side of Eye:	I don't want to go . . .
Under Eye:	I don't feel good at school . . .
Under Nose:	I'm still awesome . . .
Chin:	I acknowledge that school is stressful . . .
Collarbone:	I just want it to be over . . .
Under Arm:	I want to be done with school . . .
Top of Head:	I'd rather be doing anything else.

From Chapter 11: There's More to Explore about Grades and Report Cards

"I worry about college"

Lots of teenage girls start thinking about college as soon as they start high school. There can be pressure from parents, teachers, and even friends that creates a habit of thinking unhelpful thoughts about getting into college . . . the right college . . . the college your friend is going to.

Event	Thought	Feeling	Action
Something happens	You have a thought	That creates a feeling	You do something
My teacher said I'll never get into college	Well, he's probably right	I feel pessimistic, scared	Why bother trying/ I stop trying
We started college prep in ninth grade!	I don't even know what I want to do with my life!	I feel overwhelmed	I have trouble concentrating on studying
I had a fight with my friend who wants me to go to their college	I don't want to plan my future around them	I feel guilty that I don't want to be with my friend	I'm going to avoid thinking about it

Karate Chop: Even though my teacher said I'll never get into college, so why bother even trying, I love and accept myself.
Karate Chop: Even though my teacher is probably right, and I feel scared, I love and accept myself.
Karate Chop: Even though I'm feeling pessimistic about college, I'd rather feel more optimistic.

Eyebrow: My teacher said I won't get into college . . .
Side of Eye: He was pretty sure of himself . . .
Under Eye: I'm scared now . . .
Under Nose: Part of me wants to stop even trying . . .

Chin: My teacher's the expert, after all . . .
Collarbone: But it really is his opinion . . .
Under Arm: And not an actual fact . . .
Top of Head: What if he's wrong . . .

Eyebrow: I can't believe he said that to me . . .
Side of Eye: He's supposed to be encouraging me . . .
Under Eye: And not predicting a negative future for me . . .
Under Nose: I'm pretty angry about this . . .
Chin: I'll prove him wrong . . .
Collarbone: I'd rather be in charge of my success . . .
Under Arm: He doesn't get to decide if I get into college . . .
Top of Head: I get to decide.

Even younger girls are beginning to prep for college, so here are some tapping solutions for you if this is the place you're in:

Karate Chop: Even though I'm only in ninth grade and we are already prepping for college, I love and accept myself.
Karate Chop: Even though I don't even know what I want to do with my life, I love and accept myself.
Karate Chop: Even though I feel overwhelmed with the stress of this, I love and accept myself.
Karate Chop: Even though when I think about college my stomach churns, I love and accept myself anyway.

Eyebrow: I'm only in ninth grade . . .
Side of Eye: I don't know what I want to do with my whole life!
Under Eye: How am I supposed to know?
Under Nose: My stomach is churning about this . . .
Chin: What if I get it wrong?
Collarbone: What if I make the wrong choice?
Under Arm: This feels like too much pressure . . .
Top of Head: I don't even know where to start . . .

Eyebrow: I can't see into the future . . .
Side of Eye: But I don't need to plan everything now . . .

Under Eye: I know what subjects I like . . .
Under Nose: I know what I'm good at . . .
Chin: I'm just taking small steps right now . . .
Collarbone: I not committing to anything . . .
Under Arm: I'm going to be curious about what I want to do . . .
Top of Head: And maybe even have fun with it.

"I have no time!"

Maybe you don't have time to finish the things you need to finish, and maybe you also don't have time to do the fun things you want to do. Maybe you've discovered that you love writing, playing guitar, or grooming dogs and you would rather spend all your spare time doing that.

Karate Chop: Even though I never seem to have enough time, I love and accept myself.
Karate Chop: Even though it's hard to find time to do things I want to do, I'd rather feel easy about time.
Karate Chop: Even though I think I won't have enough time to get things done, I want time to be on my side.

Eyebrow: I never have enough time . . .
Side of Eye: Time flies when you're having fun . . .
Under Eye: Time drags when you're doing things you don't want to do . . .
Under Nose: I don't have time to do what I want . . .
Chin: I'm wasting time doing things they want . . .
Collarbone: I resent having to spend so much time on other things . . .
Under Arm: I want to feel calmer about time . . .
Top of Head: Even when things are time-consuming . . .

Eyebrow: It's hard to find time . . .
Side of Eye: My parents never have enough time . . .
Under Eye: So I might have learned it from them . . .
Under Nose: I'd rather be calmer about time . . .
Chin: I'd rather feel better about time . . .
Collarbone: I can schedule things I love to do . . .

Under Arm: And make sure I take the time to do them . . .
Top of Head: I usually get things done despite the time.

"I'm having a conflict with my teacher"

Sometimes a teacher's style and personality might be hard to be around and you might even feel like your teacher is picking on you. Maybe they said something that embarrassed you in front of the class. Maybe you even feel afraid of your teacher. Whatever your conflict with your teacher, I want to help you be calmer and more neutral about them. This is always about you feeling better, and tapping will help you feel less triggered when you're around your teacher.

Karate Chop: Even though I think they hate me, and I hate them, I love and accept myself.
Karate Chop: Even though I can't do anything right in that class, I love and accept myself.
Karate Chop: Even though they keep picking on me, I love and accept myself.

Eyebrow: I know my teacher hates me . . .
Side of Eye: They keep picking on me . . .
Under Eye: I can't do anything right . . .
Under Nose: I think I'm doing my best . . .
Chin: But I get so jumbled in that class . . .
Collarbone: I don't know why they embarrassed me . . .
Under Arm: I feel so self-conscious in that class . . .
Top of Head: I'd rather be calmer around that teacher . . .

Eyebrow: I'm afraid they'll embarrass me again . . .
Side of Eye: I would rather feel calm and confident . . .
Under Eye: And they keep picking on me . . .
Under Nose: I feel emotional around that teacher . . .
Chin: I'd rather feel calm and confident . . .
Collarbone: I'd rather be calm . . .
Under Arm: I'd rather feel strong . . .
Top of Head: I'm going to be myself.

"I have a teacher I don't respect"

Karate Chop: Even though I don't respect them, but I'm supposed to show respect, I love and respect myself.
Karate Chop: Even though I don't respect how they treat people, but they demand respect, I'd rather stay neutral.
Karate Chop: Even though that teacher thrives on embarrassing students, I'm going to be strong.
Karate Chop: Even though I don't respect the teacher because I think they're a bully, I love and accept myself.
Karate Chop: Even though they keep yelling at us and I feel uncomfortable, I love and accept myself.

Eyebrow: I don't respect the teacher . . .
Side of Eye: I think they're bullying students . . .
Under Eye: I'm supposed to respect them . . .
Under Nose: And show respect . . .
Chin: I have no respect for them . . .
Collarbone: I don't have any power . . .
Under Arm: So I'd rather be neutral with them . . .
Top of Head: And stay off their radar . . .

Eyebrow: They're always yelling at us . . .
Side of Eye: It's so stressful . . .
Under Eye: They want to hurt and embarrass students . . .
Under Nose: They're so unkind . . .
Chin: I don't want to learn from them . . .
Collarbone: They're so disrespectful to us . . .
Under Arm: I know I don't want to be like them . . .
Top of Head: I'm going to be kind and respectful instead.

Sometimes it's hard to learn

This section is for anyone who feels like some subjects are difficult to learn. It's also for you if you've been told that you have some sort of learning or behavior problem.

Karate Chop: Even though I'm upset that my teacher said I might have a problem learning, I love and accept myself.

Karate Chop: Even though I feel like I'm being judged, I love and accept myself.

Karate Chop: Even though I feel worried about my abilities now, I'd rather feel confident.

Karate Chop: Even though my parents are now worrying about my ability to learn, I love and accept myself.

Eyebrow: I'm feeling upset . . .
Side of Eye: I'm feeling judged . . .
Under Eye: I know they care . . .
Under Nose: But I feel uncomfortable . . .
Chin: I feel worried about my abilities . . .
Collarbone: I'd rather feel confident . . .
Under Arm: I know I'm doing my best . . .
Top of Head: I'd rather feel calm and confident . . .

Eyebrow: My parents are upset . . .
Side of Eye: Now they're worried about me . . .
Under Eye: What if I'm disabled . . .
Under Nose: What if I'm not . . .
Chin: I might have some challenges . . .
Collarbone: I'd rather be calmer right now . . .
Under Arm: I'm doing my best . . .
Top of Head: I'll keep doing my best.

"They tell me I have behavior problems"

Sometimes girls get labeled by something their teacher has written in a report card. I know many girls whose report cards said that they were easily distracted, for example, and their parents kept mentioning that, even years later. Here's some tapping for you if you feel like you've been labeled as having a certain type of behavior.

Karate Chop: Even though I'm hyperactive, I love and accept myself. Reminder phrase: *Hyperactive.*

Karate Chop: Even though I get distracted, I love and accept myself. Reminder phrase: *Distracted.*

Karate Chop: Even though I don't listen, I love and accept myself. Reminder phrase: *I don't listen.*

Karate Chop: Even though I keep talking, I love and accept myself. Reminder phrase: *I keep talking.*

Karate Chop: Even though I'm disorganized, I love and accept myself. Reminder phrase: *Disorganized.*

Karate Chop: Even though I'm forgetful, I love and accept myself. Reminder phrase: *Forgetful.*

Karate Chop: Even though I daydream, I love and accept myself. Reminder phrase: *Daydreaming.*

Karate Chop: Even though I'm messy, I love and accept myself. Reminder phrase: *I'm messy.*

Karate Chop: Even though I can't focus, I love and accept myself. Reminder phrase: *I can't focus.*

From Chapter 12: There's More to Explore about Bullying

"What if I'm the bully?"

I'm proud of you for reading this section and considering that you might be a bully. You might be asking yourself the question, *Is this who I want to be?* Maybe you're being bullied yourself at home by an older sibling, parent, foster parent, stepparent, or stepkids, and you think you'll feel better if you pick on others at school. Maybe it seems like a cool thing to do because you see cool kids doing it. Or maybe you think it's all in fun and you haven't really thought about how the person you're picking on may feel.

Karate Chop: Even though I thought I'd feel better if I bullied someone else, I'd like to love and forgive myself.

Karate Chop: Even though I think I'm being a bully, I will try to love and accept myself.

Karate Chop: Even though I am feeling bad about being a bully, I love and accept myself.

Karate Chop: Even though I can't believe I'm making others feel as bad as I do, I'll forgive and love myself anyway.

Eyebrow: I thought I'd feel better . . .
Side of Eye: If I picked on someone else . . .
Under Eye: I think I might be a bully . . .
Under Nose: I'm worried that I'm a bully . . .
Chin: I can't believe I'm doing that to others . . .
Collarbone: Making them feel as bad as I did . . .
Under Arm: I'd like to forgive myself . . .
Top of Head: I'd like to apologize to those I've hurt.

"I'm being gossiped about"

Gossiping is another form of bullying, and it's harmful and hurtful. Whether someone is spreading truth or lies about you, it can be painful, embarrassing, and humiliating to be talked about in a destructive way. Maybe you shared a secret with a friend and they decided at some point to spread it around the school. Or maybe someone has completely made up something about you and spread the rumor around.

Karate Chop: Even though what they're saying is so hurtful, I love and accept myself.
Karate Chop: Even though I can't believe the whole school is talking about me, I'd rather stay calm.
Karate Chop: Even though I am so embarrassed and humiliated, I love and accept myself.
Karate Chop: Even though I want to lash out and hurt them too, I love and accept myself.
Karate Chop: Even though I'm losing friends because of this, I love and accept myself.

Eyebrow: It's so hurtful . . .
Side of Eye: I thought they were my friends . . .
Under Eye: I'm so embarrassed . . .
Under Nose: I'm so humiliated . . .
Chin: I can't believe everyone knows . . .
Collarbone: I'm losing friends . . .

Under Arm: I'm so upset . . .
Top of Head: I want to lash out . . .

Eyebrow: I want to hurt them back . . .
Side of Eye: I feel so powerless . . .
Under Eye: I'd rather take back my power . . .
Under Nose: I feel so humiliated . . .
Chin: I want to feel normal again . . .
Collarbone: It's over and I'm okay . . .
Under Arm: I'm going to keep being okay . . .
Top of Head: I take back my power.

"I'm gossiping about others"

I think everyone has gossiped at some time. But when you're making up information about someone and sharing it, or you're sharing private information that you've learned about someone without that person's permission, you've moved into a dangerous area. I do mean it when I say *dangerous* because if you're starting and spreading gossip and rumors about someone, you're deliberately damaging another person's life, their reputation, their well-being.

Karate Chop: Even though I made up those rumors because I was bored, I love and accept myself and forgive myself.
Karate Chop: Even though I wanted to get revenge on them so I started that rumor, I'd like to forgive myself and love myself.
Karate Chop: Even though I thought I would seem cooler if I told that story, I love and accept myself.
Karate Chop: Even though I was feeling bad and I wanted someone else to feel worse, I think I should make amends.

Eyebrow: I was bored . . .
Side of Eye: I wanted revenge . . .
Under Eye: I wanted to seem cool . . .
Under Nose: But now I feel awful . . .
Chin: I wanted to hurt someone . . .
Collarbone: To feel better . . .

Under Arm: But I feel worse . . .
Top of Head: I think I should make amends.

Karate Chop: Even though I think I understand that I am taking my pain out on someone by bullying them, I'd rather tap and relieve my own pain.
Karate Chop: Even though I have my own pain, I don't need to give pain to others, and I forgive and love myself.
Karate Chop: Even though I feel bad about what I've done, it's not too late to change my ways.
Karate Chop: Even though I know I don't deserve to be bullied, I realize that nobody deserves it, and I forgive myself and love myself anyway.
Karate Chop: Even though I realize I've been a bully, I'd rather focus on my good qualities.

From Chapter 13: There's More to Explore about Performance

Fear of public speaking

Being afraid to speak in public is said to be the top fear in America; it's even bigger than the fear of death. Maybe you have a class presentation, a school play, a debate, or a spelling bee and have some nerves about it. I'm giving you some tapping phrases that should help you feel more comfortable in front of a group. I'm going to cover not only some of the thoughts and concerns you might be having but also some of the physical feelings people who have a fear of public speaking sometime experience.

Karate Chop: Even though I'm terrified to give my class presentation, I love and accept myself.
Karate Chop: Even though I don't want people looking at me, I love and accept myself.
Karate Chop: Even though I hate getting all that attention, I still love and accept myself.
Karate Chop: Even though my stomach feels like it's going to seize up, I love and accept myself.
Karate Chop: Even though I'm afraid to sing in front of that audience, I love and accept myself.

Karate Chop: Even though I'm afraid I'll forget my lines, I still love to perform.
Karate Chop: Even though I'm scared I'll freeze on stage, I love and accept myself.
Karate Chop: Even though I'm worried that they'll laugh at me, I love and accept myself.
Karate Chop: Even though my palms get all sweaty, I'd rather stay calm and dry.
Karate Chop: Even though I'm afraid of blushing, I love and accept myself.

Eyebrow: I have to do the presentation . . .
Side of Eye: I feel so nervous . . .
Under Eye: My stomach is squirming . . .
Under Nose: My hands are sweaty . . .
Chin: My heart races . . .
Collarbone: I'm afraid I'll turn red . . .
Under Arm: What if I blow my lines . . .
Top of Head: I'd rather feel calm and confident . . .

Eyebrow: I hate being watched . . .
Side of Eye: I don't like being the center of attention . . .
Under Eye: I'd rather be comfortable . . .
Under Nose: I'd rather feel confident . . .
Chin: I know my lines . . .
Collarbone: I did my work . . .
Under Arm: I want to feel ready . . .
Top of Head: I am calm and confident.

Keep on tapping until you're feeling calmer. If anything comes to mind, create setup statements about it. Maybe when you were younger someone made fun of you when you were doing show-and-tell. If something happened that you know launched your fear of speaking in public, do some tapping on that. Here are a few ideas:

Karate Chop: Even though they laughed at me during show-and-tell, it's over now and I love and accept myself.
Karate Chop: Even though I forgot my lines in the school play, I love and accept myself.
Karate Chop: Even though I had a lisp when I was little and people made fun of me, I'm okay now.

Karate Chop: Even though I was being loud and was told to shut up, I'd rather use my voice.

Please tap through all the points using reminder phrases that make sense for you. Now here's a story about sports performance. Even if you're not into athletics, please read and tap along.

Sports performance

Jessica's soccer coach got results and her team had a lot of wins. Jessica always worked hard and was one of the best players on the team. But during one game, Jessica made a wrong move and her coach yelled at her in front of the whole team, calling her stupid, clumsy, and lazy. She tried to shake it off but the coach's words were playing like a recording in her head that was stuck on repeat.

At her next practice, she kept making mistakes, looking clumsy, feeling stupid. Her coach was angry and yelled at her again. Her teammates couldn't believe that Jessica, a great player, was crumbling in front of them. Fortunately a teammate knew tapping and helped Jessica tap after practice.

Karate Chop: Even though Coach yelled at me in front of everyone, I still love and accept myself.
Karate Chop: Even though Coach said I'm lazy, I know I'm working hard and I love and accept myself.
Karate Chop: Even though Coach said I'm clumsy because I missed a shot, I know I'm sure-footed.
Karate Chop: Even though Coach called me stupid and that's just wrong, they had no right to speak that way and I love and respect myself too much to keep believing Coach's words.
Karate Chop: Even though I keep playing Coach's words over and over in my head, I'm turning off that player now.
Karate Chop: Even though Coach said things that made me doubt myself and even hate soccer, I'd rather remember how good I am at this.

Eyebrow: Coach lost it on me . . .
Side of Eye: I made a mistake . . .
Under Eye: And they turned on me . . .

Under Nose: Everyone makes mistakes . . .
Chin: Except I'm not allowed . . .
Collarbone: I reject the word *lazy* . . .
Under Arm: I reject the word *clumsy* . . .
Top of Head: I know I'm smart . . .

Eyebrow: I made a mistake . . .
Side of Eye: I forgive myself for the mistake . . .
Under Eye: I was doing my best . . .
Under Nose: I missed a shot . . .
Chin: It happened and it's over . . .
Collarbone: I don't need to keep reminding myself . . .
Under Arm: Of Coach's unkind and untrue words . . .
Top of Head: I'd rather be a soccer genius.

No matter what activity you participate in, you may experience something similar with your teacher, coach, mentor, or judge. Please spend time tapping until you feel your confidence return.

Creative blocks

I know for a lot of teenage girls, an early, unpleasant critique of their work can be the reason for a drop in enjoyment, confidence, and interest in continuing to pursue creative activities like writing, drawing, painting, and so on.

Lots of girls say that they were criticized at a young age for coloring outside the lines, for painting the sky orange instead of blue, or for writing a story that was unrealistic. If you were criticized early on for something you created, please tap and get that out of your system now. If you've given up creating because someone said it wasn't good enough, wasn't perfect, or wasn't realistic, I want you to be able to get the magic back.

Karate Chop: Even though I colored outside the lines, I was only four and I love and accept myself.
Karate Chop: Even though I was yelled at for painting the sky orange instead of blue, I know I learned to hate painting then.

Karate Chop: Even though I loved my story but my teacher said it was ridiculous, I'd rather regain my love of words and the ridiculous.

Karate Chop: Even though they said my portrait looked like a stick figure, I want to invite creativity back into my life.

Karate Chop: Even though creativity became linked with harshness, I'm going to separate the two and enjoy my creative mind.

Eyebrow: I colored outside the lines . . .
Side of Eye: I like to think outside the box . . .
Under Eye: I was too little to be critiqued . . .
Under Nose: I was just having fun drawing and painting . . .
Chin: I just wanted to create something . . .
Collarbone: But instead I gave it up . . .
Under Arm: It's okay to create things imperfectly . . .
Top of Head: That's perfectly okay . . .

Eyebrow: It's important to create . . .
Side of Eye: I'm creative and I've shut it off . . .
Under Eye: I'm a writer who hasn't been writing . . .
Under Nose: A painter who hasn't been painting . . .
Chin: I'm saying yes to my creative self . . .
Collarbone: And bringing her out to play and create . . .
Under Arm: It's time to feel free . . .
Top of Head: It's time to create.

From Chapter 14: There's More to Explore about Your Friendships

"I feel shy sometimes"

If you're feeling shy, that's normal and I'm not suggesting that you change your way of being. For some girls, their shyness gets in the way of being social, meeting new people, and having new experiences. Try tapping on the general theme of shyness and see what you notice. This is always a great way to get started, just tapping on the word that describes how you're feeling.

Karate Chop: Even though I think I'm shy, I love and accept myself.

Karate Chop: Even though my parents call me the shy one, I love and accept myself.

Karate Chop: Even though in my family it's not okay to be quiet, I love and accept myself.

Eyebrow:	I'm quiet sometimes . . .
Side of Eye:	My parents refer to me as the shy one . . .
Under Eye:	So I've been labeled shy. . . .
Under Nose:	Sometimes that's okay . . .
Chin:	People won't bother me as much . . .
Collarbone:	But I feel left out sometimes . . .
Under Arm:	I'd rather be more comfortable around certain people . . .
Top of Head:	Shy sounds weak . . .

Eyebrow:	But I like watching people . . .
Side of Eye:	I don't always have to be out there . . .
Under Eye:	I'd rather be comfortable around other people . . .
Under Nose:	They say I have to come out of my shell . . .
Chin:	It's okay if I like my shell . . .
Collarbone:	I'd rather feel more comfortable . . .
Under Arm:	I don't want to be labeled . . .
Top of Head:	I'd rather feel comfortable.

"Sometimes I blush"

Sometimes feeling shy is accompanied by some physical things happening in your body. Probably one of the most common is blushing. Blushing is uncomfortable because others can see your discomfort and sometimes interpret your blushing as meaning something.

Karate Chop: Even though I blush when I get called on in class, I love and accept myself.

Karate Chop: Even though blushing doesn't mean I have a crush on my teacher, I love and accept myself.

Karate Chop: Even though it throws me off when I feel my face get hot and red, I love and accept myself.

Eyebrow: Sometimes I blush . . .
Side of Eye: I can't control it . . .
Under Eye: It's so frustrating . . .
Under Nose: I don't know why it happens . . .
Chin: It's a sign that I'm uncomfortable . . .
Collarbone: I'd rather be comfortable . . .
Under Arm: Sometimes I'm caught off guard . . .
Top of Head: And that makes me blush too . . .

Eyebrow: I hate that people can see how I feel . . .
Side of Eye: It's around people in authority . . .
Under Eye: That I feel uncomfortable . . .
Under Nose: I'd rather be comfortable . . .
Chin: When adults in authority are around . . .
Collarbone: I'd rather be more comfortable . . .
Under Arm: Please tell my face that . . .
Top of Head: I'd rather be calm and neutral.

"I worry about peer pressure"

Part of growing up is feeling the influence of new people in your life. Negative peer pressure is about being influenced to do something that you might not typically do in hopes of gaining respect, friendship, coolness. Let's use tapping when you feel pressure from your friends to participate in a risky behavior.

Karate Chop: Even though my friend wants me to try _____, I love and accept myself.
Karate Chop: Even though I'm not sure if it's a good idea to try it, I love and accept myself.
Karate Chop: Even though if I don't try it, I'll probably not be in the group anymore, I love and respect myself too much to try something like that.
Karate Chop: Even though I really don't like feeling this pressure and it's starting to make me angry, I love and accept myself.
Karate Chop: Even though my parents don't want me to do this stuff, they did it when they were my age, and I love and accept myself.

Karate Chop: Even though my parents really don't want me to hang out with these people and it feels like they don't trust me, I love and accept myself.

Karate Chop: Even though my friends can be a little wild and I want to fit in, I'd rather be myself and I love and respect myself.

Karate Chop: Even though my friends are cool and I want to be cool, I also want to be myself while being cool.

Karate Chop: Even though they are pressuring me and the pressure doesn't feel good, I'd rather feel good and I love and respect myself.

Karate Chop: Even though my friend isn't used to hearing the word no, I'm comfortable with no.

Karate Chop: Even though my friend doesn't like hearing me say no, I'm going to follow my heart on this.

Karate Chop: Even though I want to say no and this other friend wants to say no, we can say no together.

Karate Chop: Even though they want me to do something I know is wrong, I love and accept myself.

Karate Chop: Even though I'm tempted to go along with them, I know it doesn't feel right, and maybe I should listen to my gut on this.

Karate Chop: Even though it seems dangerous to try this, I'm still strong if I say no.

Karate Chop: Even though I don't want to seem like a wimp, I also want to follow my values and I love and respect myself.

Eyebrow: My parents don't want me to do stuff like this . . .
Side of Eye: But I know they did it when they were my age . . .
Under Eye: They don't want me to make the same mistakes . . .
Under Nose: But that's hypocritical . . .
Chin: They want to limit me . . .
Collarbone: My friends want freedom . . .
Under Arm: I want freedom . . .
Top of Head: I want to respect myself . . .

Eyebrow: Friends want me to try this . . .
Side of Eye: Part of me really wants to try it . . .
Under Eye: Another part of me knows it's super wrong for me . . .
Under Nose: My parents would kill me if they knew . . .
Chin: I don't know if it's a good idea . . .
Collarbone: But I do know that it's a bad idea, actually . . .

Under Arm: I'm flattered that they asked me to . . .
Top of Head: But the stakes are pretty high . . .

Eyebrow: What if I got caught . . .
Side of Eye: What if I got hurt . . .
Under Eye: What if someone else was hurt . . .
Under Nose: It might be fun though . . .
Chin: And they really want me to . . .
Collarbone: I don't want to be a wimp . . .
Under Arm: But I want to do the right thing for myself . . .
Top of Head: I'd rather follow my instincts.

Tapping can help calm the conflict you're experiencing and allow you to check in with how you really feel about something. I'm not trying to solve the issue of peer pressure, but I want you to have solid tools to use when you're facing a decision. Tapping can help calm the conflict, help you see the different sides of the issue and come to your own decision that feels authentically you.

"What happened to our friendship?"

It's upsetting when a friendship changes, especially if you don't know what happened. When they're hurt and confused about a change in a friendship, a lot of girls blame themselves and worry that they did something wrong. If you find yourself in a changed friendship, I want you to take the time to tap, especially if you're confused about it.

Karate Chop: Even though I thought we were best friends but now they're friends with someone else, I love and accept myself.
Karate Chop: Even though I don't understand what happened and I thought we were friends, I love and accept myself anyway.
Karate Chop: Even though I'm confused and hurt, I love and accept myself.
Karate Chop: Even though suddenly they're giving me dirty looks and I don't understand, I still love and accept myself.
Karate Chop: Even though they're treating me like crap now, I know I deserve to be treated well.

Karate Chop: Even though they're disrespecting me, I love and respect myself too much to spend any more time thinking about it.

Karate Chop: Even though that friend keeps changing alliances, I'd rather be a loyal friend and I love and accept myself.

Eyebrow: Well, that was a shocker . . .
Side of Eye: Now they're not speaking to me . . .
Under Eye: I deserve to be treated better than that . . .
Under Nose: I'm confused and hurt . . .
Chin: Suddenly they're not my friend . . .
Collarbone: How does that even work . . .
Under Arm: That feels disrespectful . . .
Top of Head: I deserve to be treated better . . .

Eyebrow: I don't understand . . .
Side of Eye: I don't understand the dirty looks . . .
Under Eye: And being shut out . . .
Under Nose: It really hurts . . .
Chin: But I deserve better . . .
Collarbone: That's not how friends treat friends . . .
Under Arm: I deserve better . . .
Top of Head: I'm choosing friends who are a good match for me.

We're going to do more tapping on this. It's difficult when a friendship ends or friendships and alliances change. The fact is that when friendships end, it's painful for you. Let's do some tapping for the feelings you have.

"I feel confused and hurt about what happened to our friendship"

Karate Chop: Even though yesterday we were friends and today they're not speaking to me, I love and accept myself.

Karate Chop: Even though I'm so confused and I don't know what I did wrong, I love and accept myself.

Karate Chop: Even though suddenly I'm friendless and I don't know why, I love and accept myself.

Karate Chop: Even though it hurts, I deserve to be treated better than that and I love and accept myself.

Eyebrow: I'm so confused . . .
Side of Eye: What did I do wrong?
Under Eye: They won't speak to me . . .
Under Nose: Suddenly I'm shut out . . .
Chin: This really hurts . . .
Collarbone: I'm so confused . . .
Under Arm: It makes zero sense . . .
Top of Head: Suddenly I'm friendless . . .

Eyebrow: I don't know why . . .
Side of Eye: So confused . . .
Under Eye: I don't deserve to be treated this way . . .
Under Nose: I deserve to be treated with kindness . . .
Chin: I'm hurt but now I'm angry . . .
Collarbone: You don't treat people this way . . .
Under Arm: I deserve better friends . . .
Top of Head: I choose better friends.

"I feel betrayed"

No matter what age you are, being betrayed feels awful. As you get older and begin testing new kinds of relationships, you're learning about trust and trusting other people. A betrayal is a violation of your trust by another person. While it might mean that you cannot trust that person any longer, it does not mean that all people are betrayers.

Karate Chop: Even though I feel so sad, I love and accept myself.
Karate Chop: Even though I feel anxious, I love and accept myself.
Karate Chop: Even though I'm scared right now, I still love and accept myself.
Karate Chop: Even though I feel vulnerable, I love and accept myself.
Karate Chop: Even though I'm feeling so alone right now, I love and accept myself.
Karate Chop: Even though I feel very insecure right now, I love and respect myself.

Karate Chop: Even though I am so angry at them right now, I still love and accept myself.

Karate Chop: Even though I am so flipping angry right now and I can't believe they did that, I love and accept myself.

Tapping about the specifics of the betrayal will give you even more relief, so I've shared a sample of setup statements for you here. Whatever your betrayal was, please tap about it specifically.

Karate Chop: Even though I shared that deep, dark secret about myself and now everyone knows, I love and accept myself and forgive myself for trusting them.

Karate Chop: Even though they went behind my back, I love and accept myself.

Karate Chop: Even though I never thought they could betray me and it's happened, I'd rather love and accept myself.

Karate Chop: Even though I trusted them and now this happened, I love and accept myself.

Karate Chop: Even though I will never trust anyone again, I would rather not make that decision right now.

Karate Chop: Even though I feel betrayed, I love and accept myself.

Karate Chop: Even though they betrayed me, I am safe and I'm okay and I love and accept myself.

Feeling humiliated

Karate Chop: Even though I feel humiliated, I love and respect myself.

Karate Chop: Even though everyone knows what happened, I love and accept myself.

Karate Chop: Even though I'm feeling humiliated right now, I still love and accept myself.

Karate Chop: Even though everyone is looking at me, I love and accept myself.

Eyebrow: I feel humiliated . . .
Side of Eye: They humiliated me . . .
Under Eye: And did it on purpose . . .
Under Nose: I'm so self-conscious right now . . .

Chin:	I don't know what to do . . .
Collarbone:	They betrayed me . . .
Under Arm:	I feel so humiliated . . .
Top of Head:	I can't look at anyone . . .

Eyebrow:	I just want to crawl in a hole . . .
Side of Eye:	I'll never trust anyone again . . .
Under Eye:	But it was just one individual who did this . . .
Under Nose:	I know I can't trust them . . .
Chin:	I'd rather feel strong . . .
Collarbone:	That happened and it's over . . .
Under Arm:	I'd rather feel strong . . .
Top of Head:	I love and respect myself.

From Chapter 15: There's More to Explore about Your Romantic Life

"My person said I was too needy"

When you're first in a romantic relationship, you might want to be together all the time, and if you're at school together that can be easy to accomplish. But after dating for a while, if your person wants to go out on the weekend with their friends, how does that feel? It's normal, and important for each person in a relationship to maintain and nurture their other friendships and interests. If your person thinks you're expecting too much of their time, texting or calling them too much, they may accuse you of being needy. It's important to know that just because they're saying that, it doesn't mean it's true. But if it feels to you like they might be right, here's some tapping you can do to help you maintain your perspective and your confidence.

Karate Chop: Even though my person said I was too needy, I'd rather feel confident and secure.
Karate Chop: Even though now I'm worried that I'm too needy, I love and accept myself anyway.
Karate Chop: Even though they said I was too clingy, I'd rather feel secure and love and accept myself.

Eyebrow: They said I was too needy . . .
Side of Eye: What does that even mean . . .
Under Eye: So now I'm worried that I'm too needy . . .
Under Nose: I'd rather be confident and secure . . .
Chin: I didn't know I was being needy . . .
Collarbone: It hurt my feelings . . .
Under Arm: But I'd rather learn about myself . . .
Top of Head: I'd rather feel secure . . .

Eyebrow: I'd rather feel independent . . .
Side of Eye: I'd rather feel worthy . . .
Under Eye: What am I needing if I'm being too needy . . .
Under Nose: I'd rather be kinder to myself about it . . .
Chin: Maybe I do need more from a relationship . . .
Collarbone: Than my person is able to give me . . .
Under Arm: I'd rather feel confident with or without them . . .
Top of Head: I'd rather feel secure in myself.

"Why haven't they called?"

So you had a fun date with a new person on Friday night and now it's Saturday afternoon and you keep checking your phone to see if they've contacted you. You want to hear from them and to be reassured that they had a great time with you too. But the more you check your phone and text your friends to commiserate that you haven't heard from your date, the more you can spiral into the world of expecting the worst. I still remember sitting by the phone (back when they were attached to the wall), waiting for a boy to call, and I wish I hadn't wasted so much time. The truth is, you don't know why they haven't contacted you, but please tap before you turn it into a calamity.

Karate Chop: Even though they haven't called to say how much fun they had with me, I love and accept myself.
Karate Chop: Even though I'm thinking they regret our date, I'd rather not jump to such a huge conclusion.
Karate Chop: Even though I've not heard from them, it's possible that they have other stuff to do.
Karate Chop: Even though they've not called, I've not called them either.

Karate Chop: Even though I really want them to like me, I want to feel calm and confident in myself.

Eyebrow: I'm just waiting to hear from them . . .
Side of Eye: I'm putting everything on hold in case they call . . .
Under Eye: I'm worried they didn't have a good time . . .
Under Nose: I'm thinking the worst after one date . . .
Chin: That's too much stress for me . . .
Collarbone: I'd rather be calm and confident . . .
Under Arm: I like them and had a good time . . .
Top of Head: I hope they like me and had a good time . . .

Eyebrow: Beyond that, there's not much I can do right now . . .
Side of Eye: I'd rather not read into them not calling . . .
Under Eye: They never said they'd call . . .
Under Nose: I was hoping for a romantic gesture . . .
Chin: And a date tonight . . .
Collarbone: But I'd rather not obsess . . .
Under Arm: I have important things to do . . .
Top of Head: I'm going to stay calm and confident.

"My person is acting jealous"

We've all experienced jealousy, probably beginning in childhood when the neighbor kid got a toy we wanted. In romantic relationships, jealousy can at first feel flattering if your person is showing a lot of interest in you, not wanting you to spend time with other people. But if your person has a negative reaction to your giving attention to a friend, an activity, or a family member, it might be important to pay attention in case this is a warning sign of possessive, even potentially aggressive behavior.

Karate Chop: Even though it's flattering that they want to be around me all the time, I love and accept myself.
Karate Chop: Even though they complained that I was talking to my friend, I love and accept myself.
Karate Chop: Even though I'm feeling uncomfortable, I'm going to pay attention to how I feel.

Karate Chop: Even though I thought I liked that attention, I am my own person.

Eyebrow: At first their attention was flattering . . .
Side of Eye: But I'm just talking to my longtime friend . . .
Under Eye: And they get jealous . . .
Under Nose: I feel like I'm doing something wrong . . .
Chin: But I need to talk to my friends . . .
Collarbone: Without feeling bad, or hiding it . . .
Under Arm: I need to pay attention to their behavior . . .
Top of Head: And make sure they're not being too weird.

From Chapter 16: There's More to Explore about Sex

"I'm curious about these sexual feelings"

Having sexual feelings and sensations can be unsettling and confusing—even if the feelings are pleasant! So make sure you do some tapping on your feelings and thoughts about this.

Karate Chop: Even though I'm experiencing physical feelings, I'm normal and I love and accept myself.
Karate Chop: Even though I'm having physical sensations, I'm okay and I love and accept myself.
Karate Chop: Even though I'm feeling confused about these feelings, I love and accept myself.

Eyebrow: I'm having these physical feelings . . .
Side of Eye: I'm normal . . .
Under Eye: I'm confused by these feelings . . .
Under Nose: They're normal and I'm normal . . .
Chin: It's part of growing up . . .
Collarbone: To have these feelings . . .
Under Arm: I accept myself . . .
Top of Head: I accept these feelings.

Don't compare yourself to your friends when it comes to sex

Your thoughts and feelings about sex are your own, and while you might be talking to your friends about sex, please be aware that you're always in charge. Some girls may seem like they know more about sex, or even have experience with sex, but please do not compare yourself to them. They're where they are regarding sex and you're in charge of being wherever you are. Here are some tapping solutions for you.

Karate Chop: Even though my friends seem to know more about sex than I do and I feel embarrassed, I love and accept myself.
Karate Chop: Even though they seem to have more experience with sex than I do, I love and respect myself anyway.
Karate Chop: Even though they're so comfortable talking about this stuff, I'm okay wherever I am.
Karate Chop: Even though I feel out of place regarding sex, I would rather love and accept myself where I am.

Please tap through this as often as you feel like you need it and make your own reminder phrases. Go easy on yourself and give yourself permission to approach sexual topics at your own pace.

KEEP BEING AWESOME!

Congratulations! If you've read this far, you know you've got the power to feel better, calmer, happier, and more confident—literally right at your fingertips! As I said at the start of this book, I'm thrilled to know that you have this amazing tool to help you move forward into your future with less freaking out and more awesome. But I'm *really* excited that you can use it right now, today, to unpack that stress backpack and lighten your load. Tap on anything and everything! Tap with your friends. Tap with your pets.

Speaking of your stress backpack, take a moment, tune in, and check on it right now. Notice how it feels now; if you see it in your imagination, how does it look? I bet your backpack is a little lighter; it might even be a different size, shape, and color. Maybe you're feeling so awesome that you notice it's covered in bling! Checking in with your stress backpack is an easy and even fun way to pay attention to how you're feeling about things that are happening around you. I suggest marking on your calendar, or putting a reminder in your phone, to check your backpack once a week. If the bling is getting dull and you feel like you're carrying around a bit more upset than you'd like, then hop to the index of this book and find tapping exercises for the things that are bothering you right now. Do a bit of tapping on anything that's feeling bothersome and lighten your stress load.

I hope you like the Tapfirmations that you found at the end of every chapter. I'd like to invite you to check out my Twitter and Instagram and Facebook and you will find more Tapfirmations that will keep you inspired and feeling awesome. I'll always be on the lookout for new things to tap on, and I'll be sharing new setup statements and tapping exercises, so please get connected! Turn the page to find out how.

Twitter   @TapWithChris
Instagram   @tapwithchristine
Facebook   /ChristineWheelerAuthor
Pinterest   /TapWithChris

TAPFIRMATION
I'm going to keep being awesome!

APPENDIX A FOR PARENTS

Why Your Daughter Needs This Book

Your daughter is a teenager, and she's dealing with many different kinds of pressures. In addition to experiencing joy and excitement in her life, she's going to have challenges, missteps, dramas, and hurts. That's a fact—she's going to have upsetting feelings, emotions, and experiences that interrupt and interfere with her relationships, school life, home life, and happiness. While you can't shield her from all of it, of course, you can help her through many of these upsets, and being connected and communicating with her is invaluable.

But in addition to offering your love and support, what if you could put a tool in her hands that would help her process her challenges on her own? What if you offered your daughter a tool that would enhance her self-awareness, self-sufficiency, and self-confidence?

As adults, we are aware of our own challenges and we may have developed our own coping strategies, like meditation, exercise, or hot baths. Even though a young person's challenges might be very different from ours, she needs to have a way to neutralize her stress now to keep it from building up and potentially overwhelming her.

The American Psychological Association Stress in America Survey

"While the news about American stress levels is not new, what's troubling is the stress outlook for teens in the United States. In many cases, American teens report experiences with stress that follow a similar pattern to those of adults."[2]

The American Psychological Association Stress in America Survey, conducted in August 2013, has a report entitled *Are Teens Adopting Adults' Stress Habits?* The data they collected in this survey is startling, with teens reporting that they're experiencing stress at levels that are higher than they think is healthy. They report that their stress is only increasing and they expect it to continue doing so in the next year.

Unfortunately, when compared to teenage boys, teenage girls have higher reported stress levels. On a scale of 0 to 10, girls reported an average stress level of 5.1 out of 10 in the previous month, the same score as reported by adults. Boys reported their average stress at 4.1 out of 10 in the previous month. And teenage girls are more likely to feel sad or depressed as a result of their stress, with 37 percent of girls reporting that this was the case for them compared to 23 percent of boys.

Teenage girls are also reporting feeling angry and irritable because of stress (45 percent) and on the verge of tears because of stress at least once in the previous month (44 percent). Teenage girls are reporting feeling tired (42 percent) and 39 percent reported that they found themselves eating either too much or too little because of stress. If they skipped a meal, it was usually breakfast.

Overall, teens reported that school was a major source of stress for them (83 percent). When girls were asked about sources of their stress, 68 percent of the girls surveyed said that their appearance was a source of stress. Girls often felt bad when they compared themselves to others (30 percent) and more than a third of the girls experienced significant stress about how they themselves were perceived on social media.

What's especially surprising is that the survey was conducted in the month of August and respondents (both boys and girls) were asked to report on their stress for the previous month, July. Even during summer months, 13 percent of teen respondents said that they had extreme levels of stress over the summer, rating their stress at 8, 9, or 10 on a scale of 0 to 10.

Furthermore, teenage girls found it difficult to manage their stress, and a staggering 66 percent of them reported that they believed they weren't doing a very good job of doing so. These results, to me, are shocking. According to the report, teens may not be learning healthy relaxation skills from the adults in their lives, with 62 percent of adults reporting that they manage their own stress by being in front of a screen—television, computer, video game. Half of the teens surveyed indicated that they weren't confident that they were able to handle their stress.

The report indicates that teenage girls may not see that their stress has an effect on their physical and mental health, but they're "mirroring adults' high-stress lives and potentially setting themselves up for a future of chronic stress and chronic illness."[3] They're also mirroring adults' lack of stress-management ability and are often without positive role models and supportive adults to help them deal with their stress before it becomes chronic.

According to this report by the American Psychological Association, "We need to give them the skills to take control over their lives in healthy ways and allow them to grow into healthy adults."[4] I believe that giving your teenage girl this book is a huge step toward giving her the skills she needs to take control of her life. This entire book is about giving her the skill of tapping on any and every personal upset she experiences.

What This Book Is . . . and Is Not

This is a unique self-care book. It examines many of the challenges, dramas, upsets, and realities that a teenage girl faces and provides EFT tapping solutions to help her care for her own emotional well-being. It's a resource that can launch your daughter on a healthy path to ongoing and deep self-care. Your daughter will learn that what she's feeling is real and normal, and that in addition to having help and input from parents, friends, family, and trusted adults, she can have autonomy and use tapping to find her own sense of peace and calm about the issues that bother her.

By using the tools described in this book, your daughter can:

- Increase her ability to problem-solve by calming reactions that interfere with clear thinking.

- Help neutralize her negative thoughts, feelings, and beliefs.

- Increase her power and control to feel better when something is bothering her.

- Interrupt her negative thoughts, feelings, and emotions and find more peace.

EFT tapping is the best way I know that a girl can care for herself, her emotions, and her spirit. I've written this book in consultation with a teenage girl. I wanted to make sure that this book meets the teenage reader wherever she is. We acknowledge the emotions, feelings, and thoughts she's experiencing and offer simple tapping solutions for her to get relief from her upset, drama, and anxiety. EFT tapping is easy to do, and the technique itself is exactly the same, no matter what issue or upset is taking up your daughter's time and energy. This book will walk your teenage girl through the simple steps of tapping while acknowledging, accepting, and neutralizing the upsets she's currently experiencing or may have experienced in the past.

The philosophy of the book is this:

- What your daughter is feeling and experiencing is real and true for her right now.

- It's normal to have feelings, opinions, hurts, and anxieties. We acknowledge that this is normal but also that it can be very disruptive.

- The principle of EFT tapping is to acknowledge and accept the emotions and feelings as they currently appear.

- By tapping the acupuncture points with fingertips, we are giving a mini-emotional-acupuncture treatment on the specific disruptive feelings and emotions.

· ·

CASSIDY'S COMMENT

I believe that all teens should have a chance to try out EFT tapping. Whether it's for anxiety, stress, nerves, or out-of-control worrying, I'm confident that tapping will help your kids tremendously and bring down those awful feelings that everyone gets regardless of the reason.

· ·

About Emotional Freedom Techniques (EFT) Tapping

For more than two decades people of all ages, all over the world, have used EFT tapping successfully to reduce or eliminate chronic physical pain and emotional upset. It has become one of the top self-healing tools in the world because it's easy to do and has no known side effects, and because thousands of case studies have documented that it works. In more recent years, EFT tapping has been used by war veterans to alleviate symptoms associated with PTSD (post-traumatic stress disorder).

If you've had any experience with acupuncture, you know that for thousands of years practitioners of Traditional Chinese Medicine used tiny needles to stimulate specific points along channels in the body called *meridians*. Now we can simply use our fingertips to physically tap on specific meridian points to achieve calming benefits. It's so easy to do, and in fact we've always touched or tapped on different spots on the body to soothe ourselves when we're upset. For example, when you put your hands on your face in response to a shock or bad news, you're unknowingly putting pressure on some of the same acupuncture points that I talk about in this book. So it's a very natural, safe, effective, and efficient way for anybody to achieve relief. And it's especially useful for teenage girls who are experimenting with their independence because it gives them a way to take charge of their own well-being.

I first learned Emotional Freedom Techniques (EFT) tapping in 1999 when I was going through a very challenging time. My father had just died, and I was working in an aggravating job with unrelenting demands. Every day felt like a blow to my system and I knew that pressure was building and causing physical problems, but I didn't know how to get relief. So I left my job. But simply being away from that work environment didn't give me relief.

Then I learned EFT tapping and finally felt a reduction in my anxiety and depression. I didn't know why I felt better, I just knew that EFT tapping allowed me to resolve my negative thinking and physical pain, and I found a new job within a couple of weeks of learning tapping. I studied EFT tapping extensively and tapped successfully with countless friends, family, and acquaintances until I felt ready to launch my private practice as an EFT practitioner in 2002.

Fight or flight

In those early years, the most we knew about how tapping worked was that it resolved a disruption in the energy system. We said it was like emotional acupuncture without needles. We knew it worked, even if we didn't know exactly how, so we kept tapping with people on any problem that presented itself. Fast-forward a dozen years and research is finally offering some explanation as to why tapping on meridian acupuncture points may offer stress relief.

Of course you've heard of the fight-or-flight response: your body's primitive safety mechanism intended to prepare you to react to imminent danger. Your heart starts racing and adrenaline shoots into your system because your brain believes you're under threat. So now you're ready to run or to stand and fight. However, there's no pterodactyl, bear, or hatchet murderer. In fact, you're in no actual physical danger. But for some reason, your body and brain believe you're under attack.

What researchers are putting together by studying brain scans is that somehow, stimulating acupuncture points soothes the parts of the brain associated with fear.

Tapping can interrupt the false danger signals caused by daily events, allowing your body and mind to calm and more accurately perceive your surroundings.

The bottom line is that tapping calms the stress response, allowing you to feel better. I've been describing EFT this way for 15 years because I experienced the results myself, I saw the results in my own clients, and I read about people all over the world who felt better after doing EFT tapping.

Now we have scientific proof

A randomized controlled trial studied the effects of EFT tapping on the psychological symptoms and blood cortisol (the stress hormone) on a group of participants who experienced one hour of EFT tapping. This group was compared to a group who received an hour of cognitive therapy and the control group who received no intervention. There was a significant drop in the cortisol levels in the group who received EFT tapping, with an average reduction of 24 percent. Some people in the EFT tapping group had a drop in their cortisol levels of as much as 50 percent. The other groups had no significant reduction in their cortisol levels.[5]

I tell my clients who are experiencing unease in their lives that we know cortisol is the stress hormone, so if they do some tapping for an hour, they will be taking action to reduce their cortisol levels. Yes, they'll feel better emotionally, but they will also make an impact on their bodies' chemistry.

In his *New York Times* best-selling book *The Tapping Solution*, Nick Ortner does a perfect job discussing the science of tapping. I recommend reading it for great information and to have your own tapping experience.

Why I'm Writing This Book Now

I've done thousands of sessions with people using EFT tapping to help them alleviate current physical, emotional, and spiritual pain. As an EFT practitioner, my role is to help individuals uncover the past roots of current problems. In my experience working with adults who have fears, phobias, panic, and anxiety, for example, most of them experienced some kind of unresolved upset, trauma, shock, or emotional disruption in their childhood or teenage years.

When I say *unresolved upset*, I mean that something upsetting happened and they never processed, neutralized, or "got over" it. As an adult, can you think of anything that happened in childhood or in your teenage years that you really never got over? When you think of that upsetting event or person, how does it feel in your body? Do any emotions come up even now, years later?

I've written a special section for you at the end of this book so that you can gain benefits of applying EFT now, as an adult, to upsets from your own teenage years.

My intention is that this book helps teenage girls resolve hurts, heartaches, betrayals, embarrassments, and humiliations, as well as feelings about parental divorce or arguments, so they don't carry the weight of that distress into adulthood.

My view for the future is that every teenage girl has and uses the tools described in this book to achieve peace, joy, and happiness each day. I hope she will become so familiar and comfortable with EFT tapping that when she experiences something that leaves her upset, she'll be able to use this tool to release her distress immediately. My hope is that she will go forward in her life without carrying the burden of trauma, upset, disappointment, anger, and frustration that is so common among young people today. My hope is that your teenage daughter will live a life unhindered by worry, anxiety, guilt, and regret and become a joyful, healthy, peaceful, thriving adult. And my hope is that you as her caregiver will have more peace of mind and confidence in her well-being.

How to Help Your Daughter Use This Book

Please remember that this book is written for your daughter, to give her tools and tapping solutions to have with her when she feels challenged by things going on in her life. Tapping works, and we want her to have the opportunity to try out these techniques, get comfortable with them so that she has them at her fingertips when she needs them most. Her comfort with tapping will result in more peace in her life, and ultimately in your life, because you'll know she has a tool to help her feel better even if you can't. This book is not about "fixing" her, so please think of the book as a gift for her, an empowering resource written with the intention of helping her calm her tension and unleash her awesomeness.

My friend Terri Tatchell, an Academy Award–nominated screenwriter, a restaurateur, and the person who suggested I write this book, has some suggestions on the following pages for tapping with your daughter.

Tap and drive

Life with a teenage girl can be incredibly hectic and last-minute. Often a drive to school, social event, sporting event, or performance can be the perfect time to check in and get her tapping. I've noticed two benefits to the quick and focused intensity in the car: 1) If you get her to rate the intensity of her anxiety, tap, then check the number again, tap again, then check the number a third time, she'll quickly realize that even if there isn't enough time to make big progress on the drive, she has the power to manage her own anxiety. 2) She'll feel understood. Tap together (one hand on the wheel) and the empathy you feel for her (perhaps overdramatized) situation will bring you closer.

Text a tap

If you know your daughter is going to have a big test at a certain time, send a text: "Good luck with your test and remember to tap tap tap tap." She'll know you care, and a quick tap to the side of the hand before she begins will do wonders.

Teen angst

When your daughter is having a meltdown about something you would normally roll your eyes at, try tapping with her instead. She will feel understood and supported by you and it is the hyperexaggerated emotions that are the easiest to tap out! You will both benefit.

Teach by example

Embrace tapping in your life. Whether she tells you or not, nothing hurts your daughter more than seeing her mom in distress. Let her see how you use this tool to navigate challenges and take control. Ask her for help with the tapping dialogue or setup statements as she sees your situation. Sometimes they see us more clearly than we see ourselves.

Dialogue

You can start by creating setup statements that reflect what you think her concerns are. Then offer for her to take the dialogue over. You will learn a lot about her.

Tap your pets

This is fun and effective and less personal. If your pet is experiencing nervousness, upset, or pet angst, have your teenage girl tap on the pet. The tapping phrases can reflect what your girl thinks your pet is feeling or thinking. Of course she'll do anything to help the pet feel better, and in exchange, she might be more willing to tap for herself more often. And she'll probably get some relief herself because she's likely to inject wording that reflects her own thoughts and feelings.

Tapping humor

While tapping isn't a joke, let's face it—it looks funny. Embrace the humor and remember the secret side-hand tap (karate chop point) when in public.

Encourage tapping, discourage teasing about tapping

Please remember that tapping isn't homework, and it's not a punishment; it's a positive, energizing technique that can really change how your daughter deals with the challenges in her life. It's important to encourage tapping in your household. I encourage laughing about how weird tapping is (I know how weird it is even after 15 years of doing it!). I ask you to please avoid laughing at your daughter as she uses tapping and please discourage other family members from laughing at the both of you tapping. I know that sounds like a no-brainer, but the last thing a teenage girl wants is to be laughed at. Making sure home is a mockery-free zone is important so she can feel safe and comfortable using this technique.

The Stress in America study indicated that teenage girls aren't confident that they can deal with their stress effectively and that they often don't have positive role models at home for practicing relaxation. By tapping yourself and encouraging tapping in your home, you're helping to change the effects of stress in the people you love.

APPENDIX B FOR PARENTS

How to Use This Book to Help Yourself

In Appendix A for Parents I talked about the Stress in America study, which shared the shocking result that teenage girls have a similar stress score to adults' (5.1 out of 10) when asked to rate their everyday stress. I believe that adult stress is a product, in part, of unresolved childhood and teenage stress. Of course there are stressors that you experience today that you didn't have in your teenage years.

If you've read Part One of the book, you'll remember that I described stress as something you store away in your "backpack," and you're wearing that backpack of stress all the time. Using EFT tapping helps you empty out the stress that is accumulating in it, giving you a lighter load to carry forward in your life.

What I believe and know from experience is that your current stress gets packed in your backpack on top of unresolved past stress. So if you had any of the upsetting experiences that I've written about in this book when you were a teenager and you've not resolved them, they're still lingering in your backpack. They're still causing stress and they may even be creating some health problems for you. When upsetting or traumatic things happen, I don't believe you just get over them. I believe they get stuck in your backpack. When new experiences take place, your brain (amygdala) searches in your backpack for a similar experience and brings forward the thoughts, feelings, and images associated with that old wound.

So when your daughter comes to you because she has had her heart broken and she's crying and distraught, it's entirely possible that your brain goes searching in your own backpack to find how you felt about your own first heartbreak. Then not only are you dealing with your distraught daughter, you're feeling your own heartbreak again.

And on top of that, you may inadvertently be asking your hurting daughter to give you comfort when she's looking to you to comfort *her*.

If you're a father reading this, you haven't had the experience of being a teenage girl, but you may still be carrying unresolved stress from your own teenage years. Either way, if your daughter's emotional upsets trigger your unresolved emotional upsets, are you able to be completely there for her? It's not your fault and there is no judgment, it's not selfishness or self-involvement. Your brain is going to find those old issues for you, and while it's uncomfortable, it's an opportunity to finally resolve your own teenage hurts, disappointments, and upsets. Release your own unresolved issues so that you can be the best parent you can be, unhindered by having your own teenage traumas activated and agitated. I'm going to show you how to do that.

How to Use This Book for You

If you've been reading Nick Ortner's and Jessica Ortner's *Tapping Solution* books, I'll assume that you've been doing some tapping on your own and you've got a good grasp of it. But if you're coming into the world of tapping for the first time, you can scoot over to Chapter 2 and learn what you need to know to start using this book for yourself. If you want some wonderful and in-depth information about tapping, you will love the *Tapping Solution* books. For more information, visit www.thetapping solution.com.

I want you to grab your own notebook, journal, or paper and pen and ideally your own copy of this book. I do encourage writing in the book and making it your own, so if your daughter has already marked up her copy with private notes, you'll want your own.

If you have your own copy, please scan the Table of Contents and the Index to see the range of topics I've written about in the book. In the Index, a page number in boldface means there's a tapping script about that issue on that page. There are about a hundred of them. Take a couple of deep breaths and imagine your own high school years, then make a note of any issues that catch your eye. Maybe your parents divorced when you were a teenage girl. Mark that page, or write the topic and page number in your journal.

When you've chosen a topic to tap on, I want you to focus your attention on your own experience and write down in your notebook, on a scale of 0 to 10, how upsetting it is to you *now*. Even though it happened a long time ago, just thinking about it now can bring up the upset of it. And EFT tapping has been proven to reduce the current upset *and* the past upset and to give you more peace in the present.

As you think about the past upset, I want you to write down any names, details, smells, even sounds that come to mind. Then I want you to follow the tapping sequence provided, adding your own names, words, description. After you've completed a round, please check your level of intensity again and write the number down. Remember you're measuring your upset *now* when you think of that past event.

Here's what might happen: you're tapping away, thinking about that old upset and you remember another one that is similar but involves different people. This is how your amygdala unpacks the upsets that it's stored together. A simple example is that if you're tapping on your first heartbreak, as you begin to feel soothed, your second or third heartbreak might pop to the surface. It's like layers of an onion: you peel back and soothe the layers of heartache. Follow the same tapping process for any issue that shows up.

Tapping for yourself not only reduces your own stress, it sets a great example for your daughter and others in your family. Another wonderful by-product is that your own issues will not get as triggered when you're witnessing your daughter go through things. You'll be able to be more present for her, be even more compassionate when she shares her stories with you.

Are you a worrier?

I've worked with countless women over the years who described themselves as worrywarts, worriers, fusspots, and so on. I always ask, "Who taught you to worry?" A shocking number of women tell me their mothers taught them to worry. I think of it like this: Mom broadcasts her energy of worry and her daughter picks up the signal, takes up the worry banner, and runs with it.

Many of the same women tell me they don't want their children to inherit their "worry gene." If that describes you, spend as much time as you need tapping about worrying. If you've been worrying a long time, make sure you give tapping some time to interfere with this old habit. Keep at it and I know you'll feel better.

Another great reason to tap on your own worries is that teenage girls find it difficult to navigate their parents' worry. If your daughter is excited about something but you're worried that she'll have a bad outcome, you're contributing an unhelpful energy and unhelpful thinking into the scenario. Worry is unhelpful. Teenage girls read their mothers' worry as mistrust of them, their skills, and their ability to accomplish something. One of the best ways to enhance your relationship with your daughter is to calm your own worries about her.

If you're worried that something unpleasant that happened to you will also happen to your daughter, please tap that worry out of your system. Here is some tapping about that specific issue, but I believe your worry is active about your daughter because your upset about what happened to you is still unresolved. Spend some time tapping on that specific event until you feel some relief. As a result your worry about your daughter should subside. Either way, please do the following tapping exercise.

Karate Chop: Even though that happened to me when I was her age, it doesn't mean it will happen to her.

Karate Chop: Even though I worry that it will happen to her, I'd rather release that old issue now.

Karate Chop: Even though that happened, it's over and I don't need to watch out for it happening to her.

Karate Chop: Even though that happened, it's over and I'm okay and she'll be okay too.

Tapping when you get triggered

In addition to going through the Table of Contents and the Index, you might have a clear memory of an interaction with your daughter when you know you were triggered by something that happened to her. Find that issue in this book and do those tapping exercises. Start by writing down a few words to describe your own experience and feelings, and write down your level of intensity right now. Tap until you feel some relief and your level of intensity number is lower.

When you're feeling more peaceful about your memory that was triggered, I want you to do the following tapping:

Karate Chop: Even though my daughter needed me but I kept thinking about my own hurt, I love and accept myself.

Karate Chop: Even though she needed me and I was distracted by my own pain, I forgive myself, I was doing my best.

Karate Chop: Even though I might have minimized her pain, I forgive myself and I love and accept myself.

Tap through all the points while repeating reminder phrases that express how you're feeling.

Tapping about your daughter

Have you ever been shocked to suddenly notice that your daughter reminds you of your ex, your mother, or your own high school bully? Maybe it is a physical resemblance, a look on her face, or her mannerisms that set you off. When your amygdala registers that resemblance, it instantly goes into your old files and dredges up thoughts, feelings, images, and beliefs, brings them forward, and dumps them at your feet.

Debra kept having arguments with her teenage daughter, Anna, who bore a striking resemblance to her father, now Debra's ex. When Debra started doing some tapping on her relationship with Anna, she realized that the look on Anna's face when she wasn't getting her way triggered Debra's unpleasant memories of her ex-husband's constant look of disapproval. Once she did lots of tapping to resolve that trigger, Debra was able to look at her daughter and just see Anna. Here's some of the tapping she did:

> **Karate Chop:** Even though when I look at Anna I feel the disapproval of my ex, I'd rather just see my daughter.
> **Karate Chop:** Even though when I look at Anna I think she's representing her father's disapproval, I love and accept myself.
> **Karate Chop:** Even though Anna is not her father yet I still see his face when I look at her, I'd rather separate these two distinct people.

Some women have trouble communicating with their teenage daughters because their behavior reminds them of a friend, an acquaintance, or a bully from their own teenage years. Please use the same tapping to resolve that trigger by adding the name of the person she's reminding you of. This will help you separate the similarities and allow you to experience your daughter as her unique self.

Tapping through an argument

If you're having a discussion with your daughter (or anyone) and you feel yourself getting upset, emotional, or frustrated, immediately start tapping. Yes, start tapping in the middle of your discussion and invite your daughter to tap as well. You both might become more calm (I know, it's weird) and your conversation can be much more productive. Also you're both able to be more present in the conversation because the tapping interrupts your brain from going to find old files about similar arguments from your past. I think of this as an easy way to get to win-win.

You can tap on all the tapping points if you feel like it. Or you can secretly tap on the fingertip points or the karate chop point on the side of your hand if you're talking with a nontapper. Doing the Butterfly Hug while talking is a great way to get relief, clarity, and even new insights. Adding tapping to your conversations will heighten your ability to reach a peaceful resolution.

When something serious or upsetting happens and you can't help but go on a tirade about something she's done or not done, you need to start tapping. Ultimately you want to have peace with your daughter. And even though you might feel like you want her to know how deeply angry or hurt or upset you are, tapping while you're ranting at her can bring a resolution much more quickly. If she joins you in tapping, you may find common ground more easily.

However you decide to do so, including tapping in your family life will help to bring peace, increase harmony, and enhance joy.

NOTES

1. J. S. Middlebrooks and N. C. Audagne, "The Effects of Childhood Stress on Health across the Lifespan," Centers for Disease Control and Prevention, 2008, http://health-equity.pitt.edu/932/1/Childhood_Stress.pdf.

2. American Psychological Association, "Stress in America: Are Teens Adopting Adults' Stress Habits?" press release, February 11, 2014, apa.org.

3. Ibid.

4. Ibid.

5. D. Church, G. Yount, and A. Brooks, "The Effect of Emotional Freedom Technique (EFT) on Stress Biochemistry: A Randomized Controlled Trial," *Journal of Nervous and Mental Disease* 200, no. 10 (October 2012), 891–896.

INDEX

ACKNOWLEDGMENTS

Working on this book has been one of the most rewarding experiences of my life and I love having this opportunity to word-hug the amazing people who helped to light my path. My favorite person on the planet, Ken Lawson, I love that you've been at my side for each moment of this adventure, making sure I've always had an inspiring and fun haven to work in and play in. Thank you for filling my life with love, kindness, laughter, ridiculousness, and snacks. I love you. My sister, Anne, your presence in my life fills me up. Thank you for giving me insight and perspective on my own teenage years, and for always knowing when I needed a boost.

To my super talented Teen Consultant, Cassidy, I am so honored that you've shared your wonderful voice, your humor, and your valuable wisdom with the girls reading this book. I've loved having your input from the very first outline of "stuff girls should tap on", to the last "Cassidy's Comment". Your words make this book complete.

To my incredible friend, Terri Tatchell, thank you for suggesting that I write a book for girls so they can have tapping in their lives. I'm so glad I listened to you! You are the catalyst for this book, my first reader, and my first online purchaser. I am so grateful for your insights, ideas, encouragement, and excitement; your belief in me gave me the push I needed.

Oh, Nick Ortner, I will never forget your life-changing e-mail, suggesting that this would make a great Tapping Solution book. I appreciate your kindness, your generosity, and your sincere, deep desire to make a difference in the world. Thank you for writing the perfect foreword for my book and for illuminating the path that has led me into your Tapping Solution world and into the wonderful world of Hay House!

I feel so blessed and gleeful to be a part of the love-filled world of Hay House. Thank you so much to Patty Gift and Reid Tracy for bringing me into the publishing house of my dreams. I've been inspired by every communication, and each person on the Hay House team. I appreciate you all for investing your time and talent in this project. Thank you to my first editor, Laura Gray, for helping to create a brilliant blue-print for the book.

To my forever editor, Anne Barthel, I love that you get me! Your inspired and kind attention to every word made this a better book. Working with you has been joyful and fun and I know I'm a better writer having had this opportunity to make sentences with you!

Michelle Polizzi, thank you for your beautiful, instantly loved cover design, and Pam Homan, thank you for creating a perfect look and feel inside the book. And my excitement and gratitude continues as I work with Aurora Rosas and Lindsay McGinty, who've expanded my horizons, helping to get this book in the hands of teenage girls.

I am so grateful to my friend Janet Conner, whose teachings helped me get into a place of connectedness so that all my writing has become a spiritual practice. And thank you for knowing who would be the perfect agent for me, and for making sure we connected.

To my agent, Jo Ann Deck; I feel like I dreamed you. You've been my perfect guide and trusted mentor. Thank you for helping me navigate this exciting world!

I appreciate the encouragement of friends and family who've been excited for me along the way, especially my dear friend Therese Dorer for being my strong pillar of love, fun, and spiritual insight. To my great friend Rob, thank you for reminding me that all of this is my "new normal."

I am so proud of the teenage girls I've worked with over the years who have used tapping so enthusiastically, and who keep being awesome. Thank you for being an inspiration.

ABOUT THE AUTHOR

Christine Wheeler MA is the co-author of *IBS for Dummies* (Wiley) and the *IBS Cookbook for Dummies* (Wiley). In *IBS for Dummies* she introduced EFT tapping to people with IBS, this being one of the first mainstream health books to include significant and highly referenced information about EFT as a soothing option for the emotional and physical discomfort associated with this illness.

Christine has been an Emotional Freedom Techniques (EFT) Tapping practitioner in private practice since 2002. From her home base in Vancouver, Canada, she has worked with thousands of people one-on-one, using EFT tapping to help them alleviate physical, emotional and spiritual challenges, find peace, and live with hope and joy.

She has also taught EFT to parents, school counsellors, and youth addictions counsellors in order to put this unique self-help tool into the hands of people who are caregivers for youth. For several years, she has served on the board of directors of Some Assembly Arts Society, in Vancouver, British Columbia, a non-profit society formed as a way for diverse populations of youth and artists to collaborate on the creation of new and original plays based on content of importance and relevance to youth and involving issues facing teens today.

www.christinewheeler.com

NOTES

NOTES

NOTES

NOTES

HAY HOUSE

Look within

Join the conversation about latest products,
events, exclusive offers and more.

f Hay House UK

🐦 @HayHouseUK

📷 @hayhouseuk

♥ healyourlife.com

We'd love to hear from you!